The MAGIC of UNICORNS

Also by Diana Cooper and Published by Hay House

Books

Dragons (2018)

The Archangel Guide to the Animal World (2017)

The Archangel Guide to Enlightenment and Mastery (2016)

The Archangel Guide to Ascension (2015)

Venus: A Diary of a Puppy and Her Angel (2014)

Oracle Card Decks

Archangel Animal Oracle Cards (2019)

Dragon Oracle Cards (2017)

Guided Visualizations (available in Audio Digital Download Format)

The Magic of Unicorns (2020)

Dragons: Visualizations to Connect with Your Celestial Guardians (2018)

The Archangel Guide to Enlightenment and Mastery: Visualizations for Living in the Fifth Dimension (2016)

The Archangel Guide to Ascension: Visualizations to Assist Your Journey to the Light (2015)

THE
MAGIC OF
UNICORNS

Help and Healing from the Heavenly Realms

DIANA COOPER

HAY HOUSE

Carlsbad, California • New York City
London • Sydney • New Delhi

Published in the United Kingdom by:
Hay House UK Ltd, The Sixth Floor, Watson House
54 Baker Street, London W1U 7BU
Tel: +44 (0)20 3927 7290; www.hayhouse.co.uk

Published in the United States of America by:
Hay House LLC, PO Box 5100, Carlsbad, CA 92018-5100
Tel: (1) 760 431 7695 or (800) 654 5126
www.hayhouse.com

Published in Australia by:
Hay House Australia Publishing Pty Ltd, 18/36 Ralph St, Alexandria NSW
2015
Tel: (61) 2 9669 4299; www.hayhouse.com.au

Published in India by:
Hay House Publishers (India) Pvt Ltd, Muskaan Complex,
Plot No.3, B-2, Vasant Kunj, New Delhi 110 070
Tel: (91) 11 4176 1620; www.hayhouse.co.in

A catalogue record for this book is available from the British Library.

Interior illustrations: 1, 127, 175, 207, © Marjolein Kruijt; all other images Shutterstock

Tradepaper ISBN: 978-1-4019-6119-0
E-book ISBN: 978-1-78817-432-9

13 12 11 10 9 8 7 6 5 4

Printed in the United States of America

This product uses responsibly sourced papers and/or recycled materials. For more information, see www.hayhouse.com.

I am the purest of the pure.
I hold all in love so sure.
I am benevolence and grace.
I spread light to the human race.
As your unicorn
so bright,
Let me be your guiding light.

YOUR UNICORN

Contents

Introduction

It is many years since my unicorn first came to me and touched me with its pure white energy. I remember the jolt of delight I felt as I realized it was a unicorn, for at that time I thought, as did many people, that unicorns were creatures of myth and legend. Although I was aware that ancient stories were perpetuated because psychics and mystics described the beings they saw in other dimensions, I had never given unicorns credence. But then, in the same way that angels drew themselves to my attention by appearing before me and telepathically communicating with me, unicorns were asking me to tell people about them. I was honoured and delighted to be one of their messengers.

At that time, 12 years ago, these illumined beings were starting to come back to Earth for the first time since the decline of Atlantis. They were looking for people who had a light over their head that meant they were in service. When such people were ready, a unicorn would approach them and assist them in achieving their visions. Often these individuals were totally unaware of the great inspiration and assistance they were receiving.

The unicorns told me then that they were fully of the angelic realms and were seventh-dimensional ascended horses.

I now know that was information tailored to the level I was at then. Unicorns are so much more! Since I wrote my first unicorn book, *The Wonder of Unicorns*, under their guidance, I have learned a vast amount more about illumined unicorns, and I am looking forward to sharing it in this book. Unicorns are awesome beyond imagining.

The frequency of the world is much higher now than it was when they first came to me. The vibration of the planet has risen incredibly in the past decade, for many high-frequency energies have flowed in to touch people. Great portals have opened. Supermoons have brought a huge influx of Divine Feminine light to dissolve old masculine paradigms. Dragons have returned *en masse* to add their love and ancient wisdom. Highly evolved angels, masters and star beings have arrived from other planets and universes to beam their special energies onto us. The aim is to ensure the planet and all on her are fifth-dimensional by the start of the new Golden Age in 2032.

And at last we are ready to receive the attention of huge numbers of unicorns, known as the purest of the pure, for they carry Source love and light. They have served the universes for aeons and shimmer with the radiant white that contains all the colours.

As people become more spiritual, they can easily link to seventh-dimensional unicorns. Many are rapidly raising their vibration and starting to communicate with these extraordinary beings at a ninth-dimensional level. Almost unbelievably, some lightworkers are radiating such a bright light that they are being touched by 10th-dimensional unicorns.

All unicorns help to enlighten us and enable us to ascend to higher dimensions, so the possibility for total transformation is now available if we ask for it.

Unicorns are everywhere, and if you are reading this, you are ready to meet them. If you are already connected to them, this book will prepare you to work with them much more deeply. It will take you on a journey with them into the highest frequencies currently available. I hope you will relax and enjoy it.

Some of the visualizations are very long. Don't try to remember them. Just read them, closing your eyes when you feel the need and then opening them and reading a little more. This will impact on your consciousness and shifts will happen within you.

Many people find it helpful to keep a unicorn journal. This is a special exercise book in which you write your thoughts and experiences. When you jot down your unicorn dreams and visualizations with any messages you receive, it enables you to anchor the memories. It also keeps them alive for you when you read your journal later. You may like to decorate your unicorn journal to make it beautiful and unique.

Remember that as soon as it sees your light, your personal unicorn will shower you with blessings and healing. Be open and receptive to the joy that is available.

*Unicorns bring a message of hope and remind us
to stay positive as we prepare for a golden future.*

PART I

AN INTRODUCTION
TO UNICORNS

CHAPTER 1

The History
of Unicorns

A t cosmic levels, unicorns are a group consciousness.
Imagine an intense cloud of pure diamond-white light
floating round the universe spreading joy and blessings. That is
the unicorn energy.

How did it become individual unicorns? It started in
Lemuria, which was the fourth Golden Age on this planet.
The beings of that time were etheric and did not have a body.
They were a group consciousness, rather like the purest unicorn
energy. When that civilization ended, they individuated. They
then petitioned Source for physical bodies. They wanted to
experience the senses of touch, taste and smell and to take
responsibility for a body. Source granted this petition and that
was when the great experiment of Atlantis was conceived. This
was intended to offer those brave souls who took part huge
opportunities for spiritual growth. It also gave them the chance
to experience free will.

Unicorns in Atlantis

The unicorn energy, so pure and full of love that it could not envisage anything beyond its beautiful light, watched the transition from etheric Lemurian consciousness to physical Atlantean bodies with interest. Atlantis was reconfigured five times and each time the experiment had to be terminated because the frequency of the participants became too low. The unicorn energy observed it all. Finally, during the fifth configuration of Atlantis, the extraordinary Golden Age arose. This time, beings from all over the universes incarnated. All vibrated at the upper levels of the fifth dimension and lived in open-hearted oneness.

These Golden Age Atlanteans radiated such beautiful light that the unicorn energy approached and supported them in maintaining their high frequency. At this point, like the Lemurians, the unicorn energy offered to individuate into physical bodies to help and serve these high-frequency humans. Source and the Intergalactic Council chose the horse shape because it was stable and strong. So, the unicorn energy incarnated as pure white, fully enlightened horses, with their brow chakra open, so that a spiralling horn of light shone from it.

In its purest form, the unicorn energy is 12th-dimensional and resides beyond the Stargate of Lyra. It is impossible for humanity to access this ineffable frequency, so the unicorns who descended to help the Atlanteans of the Golden Era stepped their frequency down through Lakumay, the ascended aspect of Sirius.

When they incarnated, they believed they would be free, and at first they were. They were loved and honoured. People asked for their help and were grateful for it. These pure white horses, with their great strength, volunteered to assist their human friends with heavy farming work. They also generously offered to help humans travel and were ridden bareback and directed telepathically by their riders. Even now, Native Americans ride bareback, without reins, and this is how the relationship between horses and humans was envisaged.

But then the civilization of Atlantis started to decline. The spiritual hierarchy was shocked and saddened to see these gracious creatures saddled and bridled, reined, shackled, overworked and even eaten. And many of the horses, over successive incarnations, became angry, stubborn and bitter. This held back their evolution and they no longer reflected a pure white colour.

Like humans, physical horses are subject to the spiritual laws of Earth. Once a being incarnates on this planet, it must reincarnate again and again to learn its lessons. This continues until it becomes a perfected being. Some horses activated the Law of Cause and Effect, thus creating karma. Others, despite provocation, maintained their purity and ascended in a blaze of light. They returned to Lakumay and waited for the frequency on Earth to rise so that they could come back to help humanity. Now they help us as unicorns in spiritual bodies.

As the frequency on Earth has risen over recent years, many more horses have forgiven the humans who abused them, evolved as a result of their challenges, maintained their pure spirit and ascended once more into the unicorn realms. I know two people who have been blessed to watch their beautiful white horses pass over, become illuminated and transform into unicorns. They both described this to me as the most extraordinary and wonderful thing to see.

Unicorns Return to Earth

In 1987 the Harmonic Convergence occurred, a special line-up of planets that heralded the start of the 25-year period of purification before the Cosmic Moment in 2012. At that instant the Stargate of Lyra opened a crack and some unicorns took the opportunity to slip through and come to Earth.

In 2015 a number of things happened. The incidence of Supermoons started to increase. These are Full Moons that occur when the Moon is at its closest point to Earth in its orbit. They are truly unicorn Moons, for these amazing spiritual beings pour onto the planet when Supermoons grace us with their light.

Also, the Stargate of Lyra opened fully, allowing more very high-frequency unicorns to gain access to Earth and humanity.

Special stellar alignments, the opening of many portals, the reactivation of the Great Crystal of Atlantis and the assistance of the dragon kingdoms all meant that world-wide more people brought down their fifth-dimensional chakras and stepped onto the first rung of the ascension ladder. All of this allowed more surges of unicorn energy to flow to Earth. Suddenly people everywhere subliminally remembered them. This was reflected in the upsurge of unicorn toys and in pictures of unicorns being used in all kinds of merchandizing. Each time a person saw one, it reminded them of what they unconsciously knew and opened them up to their light.

Now, as the planet is ascending very quickly, a new wave of unicorns is gaining access to it via the Moon. They then step down through the causal chakras of those humans who are sufficiently evolved to provide a portal for their entry. I share more about this later in this book.

At last we have earned the right to be assisted by unicorns once more. Millions of people have radiated enough light to draw them to this planet again.

We are blessed that unicorns have once
more come to Earth to help us.

If you would like to make a connection with unicorn light, you can try the following exercise:

MAKING A MAGICAL CONNECTION
TO SIRIUS AND THE MOON

~ On a clear night if possible, go outside and look at the sky. Even if you cannot actually see the stars and the Moon, they will still be there and you can make an energetic connection with them.

~ Mentally say, 'I now connect to Sirius and call for unicorn light to touch me.'

~ Pause and notice how you feel.

~ Mentally say, 'I now connect to the Moon and call for unicorn light to touch me.'

~ Again pause and notice how you feel.

Whether you are aware of it or not, a thread of pure white light will have formed between you and Sirius and the Moon. Your magical connection will have been made.

CHAPTER 2

Unicorn Information

H ere's a little more basic information about unicorns.

Unicorn Forms

As great beings of light, unicorns can take any form. A unicorn
may decide to show itself to you as a light, an Orb, a diamond,
and in any colour. However, unicorns love and respect the horse
shape that was chosen for them by Source and the Intergalactic
Council, for it represents strength and freedom, so they usually
appear as pure white horses, and this is how mystic painters or
sculptors usually choose to present them.

A unicorn is fully enlightened, so the third eye in its forehead
is wide open and radiates light so bright that it appears solid
and takes the form of a spiralling horn. When a unicorn touches
you with its horn, it brings enlightenment or healing and raises
your frequency. It may download spiritual information directly
into your consciousness and may even radiate light into one or
more of your chakras to make profound changes within you.

Sometimes a unicorn pours a fountain of light over your energy fields, conferring a blessing on you.

In this book, when I refer to unicorns, I am including Pegasi and Unipegs.

What Is a Pegasus?

A Pegasus is a form of unicorn energy with a fully developed heart chakra, which becomes so open that the rays from it form etheric wings, so Pegasi are seen as pure white horses with wings. They have ascended and some of them spend time on Venus, the Cosmic Heart, when they first arrive in this universe. This helps them to develop their heart chakra. Pegasi love to enfold you in their wings of light.

What Is a Unipeg?

A Unipeg is fully evolved in mind and heart, so it has a horn of enlightenment as well as wings.

The Dimensions

People talk about the 'seventh heaven', meaning the angelic realms of glory, harmony, love and happiness. In fact they are referring to the seventh-dimensional frequency band. Huge numbers of unicorns reside at this level. Those unicorns who vibrate at ninth- and 10th-dimensional frequencies live on an even faster waveband. Their light and joy are so bright and beautiful that they are awesome. Some of them are now touching people on Earth with inconceivably pure light.

Unicorn Qualities

Unicorns have a feminine energy, though they stay in balance and help you to come into equilibrium too. They can pour wisdom, love, compassion, healing, mercy, joy, peace and all the Divine Feminine qualities into you and at the same time they can give you strength, courage, vitality, dignity, decisiveness and other qualities to push you forward and enable you to take action in the right way.

Unicorns balance your masculine
and feminine qualities.

Unicorn Healing

Unicorns are healers. Their presence soothes and calms you and raises your frequency to a level higher than that of any dis-ease. When your vibration is faster than that of an illness, the illness can no longer manifest. It has to dissolve.

In addition, unicorns' horns are like magic wands, pouring out incisive laser-like light that they can direct precisely where it is needed. They heal at every level – mental, emotional, physical and spiritual, and also at a deep and profound soul level. They can dissolve karma. All healing eventually impacts on the physical.

Unicorns raise your frequency above
that of a disease or problem.

Reconnecting People to Their Spirit

Unicorns are soul healers – they help those who have experienced loss or trauma of any kind. When a person has been deeply scarred in childhood, or even as an adult, their spirit, or part of it, may return to their soul. Unicorns are masters of retrieving these parts – a process known as 'soul retrieval'.

Unicorns awaken an energy within you that allows you to reconnect with your soul.

In addition, many high-frequency, very sensitive people are incarnating now. Some of them find it difficult to stay in their body, especially when they are surrounded by low or negative energy. As a coping mechanism, they unground themselves and their spirit withdraws slightly. Unicorns can help to bring back lost energies to reground these people in their physical body.

Unicorn Presence

Unicorns in Dreams and Meditation

It seems to me that more people nowadays are meeting their unicorn when they are asleep. If a unicorn comes into your dreams, it is very special, for it has made a connection that can have a profound impact at a soul level. I will share more about meeting your unicorn, and unicorns and dreams, later on.

Also, people are often connecting with unicorns during meditation. Many people have shared their unicorn dreams and meditations with me and I include some of them in this book.

When you experience the presence of a unicorn, however it happens to you, expect wondrous things to happen.

Baby Unicorns

Some years ago, after a psychic child told me of her experiences with a baby unicorn, I started to become aware of their joyful presence. Here is Utte's story about her connection with a baby unicorn:

There was a grove near my home in the south of France where I liked to meditate. In the middle of it was a tree shaped like the horn of a unicorn. Once I saw a big white female unicorn there, who told me that her name was Aurora. When Aurora returned on another occasion, she was followed by a baby unicorn, who was pink. Her name was Minerva, and she was learning everything from Aurora.

I often see them now, and the baby has grown up and become a lighter pink. Aurora and Minerva are always together, and whenever I need them or have something special to do, they are with me.

CHAPTER 3

An Overview of the Angelic Realms

I used to refer to the 'angelic hierarchy' until the angels pointed out that they were part of the oneness, so there was no separation and therefore no grades or levels. They reminded me that a primary schoolchild might be a pure and beautiful soul, even though it did not yet have the knowledge or experience of the head teacher. One wasn't better or more important than the other. So now I refer to the 'angelic realms'.

The Angelic Realms

Unicorns are angelic beings and hold a very high, pure light. So do angels, archangels, powers, virtues, dominions, Thrones, Cherubim and Seraphim. They all operate on different wavelengths and perform a variety of tasks.

Archangels and others in the angelic realms have evolved spiritually through trials and initiations to a high frequency.

Guardian angels vibrate at a frequency that is more in tune with humans.

Dragons, who are ancient, wise, open-hearted beings, are also of the angelic realms and are flocking to Earth now to help humanity and the planet. Their younger brethren, the elementals, such as fairies, elves, mermaids and salamanders, evolve through the angelic line too.

The Roles of Different Angelic Beings

Unicorns, angels and dragons all undertake different roles. There is some overlap, as they are all beings of wisdom, compassion and love who are here to serve. Because you as a human being have free will, they must stand aside and observe what is happening without interfering, unless you ask for assistance.

Unicorns

Unicorns are beings of pure white light who pour inspirational energy over both individuals and humanity as a whole. They range from the seventh to the 12th dimension. They do not sing, as angels do, but they hold the perfect vision for Earth.

Angels

Angels too operate through the frequency bands from the seventh to the 12th dimension. Guardian angels assist and guide individuals. Other angels look after projects, towns, countries and even stars. Currently, as the energy on Earth is rising, more of the elevated angels are stepping in to sweep us forward to ascension.

Angels watch over us or actively shine light onto us to inspire us.

Dragons

Dragons are wise, loving beings who have wings, like angels, that are extensions of their heart centre. They operate from the fourth dimension up to the highest levels. Fourth-dimensional dragons can dive into deep, dense energies and clear them, which angels and unicorns cannot do. They can also materialize and dematerialize matter. Currently, many highly evolved dragons from other star systems and galaxies have come to Earth to share their wisdom and knowledge with us.

Angels and dragons work through the heart,
while unicorns work with the soul.

The Elemental Realms

The fairies, elves, gnomes, goblins and mermaids who look after the nature kingdoms are all part of the elemental realms. They operate between the third and fifth dimensions.

Taking the analogy of a school again, the elementals are the younger siblings of the angels and unicorns. They are the kindergarten children, while the unicorns and Seraphim are the head teachers.

Fairies, who are air elementals, work with unicorns. For example, mighty unicorns may ignite a peace flame over a town to bring a feeling of safety to the inhabitants. When they have moved on, fairies will anchor that energy so that it lasts longer.

While humans have all four elements – fire, earth, air and water – in their make-up, unicorns and most archangels have only the air element. Dragons and elementals can have up to three elements.

Every creature in the cosmos is evolving. For instance, when fairies who are already fifth-dimensional move up a class, they become angels.

CHAPTER 4

Your Personal
Companions and Helpers

You have a personal unicorn, a guardian angel and a companion dragon waiting to connect with you. Who are these personal helpers?

Unicorns

When your fifth-dimensional chakras are open and activated, you start to connect to your Higher Self or soul. This is when your light really starts to shine. Unicorns scan humanity for those whose lights are on and as soon as they see that you are ready, they come to you. They maintain a high, pure energy and pour their white Source light over you.

The Role of Your Personal Unicorn

Your unicorn watches over your energy, and when you have pure intentions or a vision to help others, it immediately approaches you. As soon as your light becomes bright enough, it is with you, inspiring and illuminating you and pouring blessings over you. It works with you at a soul level, helping you fulfil your life purpose and bringing you joy and delight. If you are becoming dispirited, it will pour light over you or touch and activate your chakras in order to encourage you, and will empower and support your journey. If you nurture a desire that will bring you soul satisfaction and fulfilment, it will take this to Source for activation. It will also pour soul qualities like love, courage, understanding, wisdom and power into you to help your vision to come to fruition.

Your unicorn connects to you when you
wish to use your life to serve others.

Your unicorn is constantly shining light onto you, though it holds you in the purest love and will only send you as much light as you can cope with.

It also raises your frequency, so that you can rise above a situation if you need to. It always has the growth of your soul, your community and the world in mind and helps you see things and people from an enlightened perspective.

In the Golden Era of Atlantis, people knew their personal unicorn, so if you incarnated then you have a soul link with yours and it is waiting to reconnect to you as soon as you are ready. It may already be with you. These love links never dissolve.

Guardian Angels

Everyone has a guardian angel who stays with them throughout their soul journey, regardless of how low their frequency drops.

The Role of Your Guardian Angel

Your guardian angel looks after you and protects you. It pours unconditional love over you, whatever you do. If you have a heartfelt wish, your angel will bring it to fruition as long as your soul allows.

Your guardian angel is with you when you are born and with you when you die. It is present at your pre-life consultation. It saves you from accident or death if that is not for your highest good or part of your destiny. It holds the divine blueprint for your life and whispers guidance to you that will enable you to follow your highest path. You have the choice whether you listen to this or not! Your angel also orchestrates the coincidences and synchronicities that enable you to meet the right people and be in the right place at the right time.

Dragons

Dragons are incredibly ancient, wise, open-hearted beings. Most of them withdrew from the planet at the end of Atlantis. Some of those who belonged to Earth remained, however, and have been protecting the planet for thousands of years. Like unicorns, millions of these wise beings are now flooding back to help us. As well as our local dragons, those from many other planets and planes of existence are here now to assist people, animals and the planet.

The Role of Your Companion Dragon

Dragons are made up of the elements fire, earth, air or water, but not all together. Your companion dragon may be of one element only, usually that associated with your birth sign, but it is more likely that it is predominantly of one element, with the influence of up to two others.

Your companion dragon protects you. It looks after you when you are asleep and clears lower energies in your vicinity. It is tremendously loyal and will stay very close to you once you have made the connection to it. It will light your way.

> *Your personal unicorn, guardian angel*
> *and companion dragon all love you*
> *unconditionally and see the best in you.*

Calling for Help

Which of these helpers should you call on for help and what is the best way to do it?

For Yourself

If you are in need of help at any time, first call on dragons to clear any dense energy. Then ask angels to surround you with light and finally invoke unicorns and ask them to pour showers of white light over you.

In a Challenging Situation

Similarly, if you are facing a challenging situation, ask dragons to dive into the darkest energies and clear them. Fourth-dimensional dragons who can consume deep energies will automatically respond. Then ask angels to keep the energy around the situation as high as possible and sing in beautiful qualities, love and light.

Finally, ask unicorns to fly above the situation or location and pour pure white light over it.

If you see a challenging situation such as a natural disaster or a humanitarian crisis on television or social media, you can send in dragons to transmute the density in the land itself. Then ask angels to enfold the people there in love and hold the area in golden light. Thirdly, as above, ask unicorns to fly above the situation and pour white light over it.

To Clear a Space

When you are going somewhere, you can ask dragons in advance to clear it of any lower energies. As before, then ask angels to hold you in their light and unicorns to fly above you. You will then be in a cocoon of perfect angelic love. You can do this with your office, therapy room, classroom or any home or work space. It only takes a moment.

You can place the cocoon round yourself, someone else, a place or a situation. Here are a couple of examples:

CREATING A COCOON OF ANGELIC LIGHT FOR A SAFE JOURNEY

~ As you sit in your vehicle, whether that is a car, boat, train, plane or something else, call in dragons and see or sense them arriving.

~ Ask one of them to fly in front of you, clearing lower energies, while the others fly in formation round you.

~ Call in angels. Be aware of golden angels holding the energy round the vehicle you are in.

~ Invoke unicorns. See them above you, blessing your journey with a stream of white light.

~ You are in a cocoon of wondrous angelic beings. Relax and trust that you are totally protected.

~ Remember to thank them when you reach your destination.

CREATING A COCOON OF ANGELIC LIGHT TO HEAL A WAR ZONE

When you meditate or visualize, it is important that the space around you is clean and light. Just as dirt and dust accumulate in corners, so do psychic cobwebs. When you are not meditating on the move, here are some things you can do to ensure your room is sparkling clean:

~ Ask air dragons to blow out any lower vibrations and blow in higher ones.

~ Use singing bowls or cymbals to clear old energies.

~ Clap and 'om' into the corners. This breaks up stuck energy and replaces it with new.

~ Place amethyst crystals in the corners.

To create a cocoon of angelic light around a war zone:

~ Imagine the place in your mind's eye.

~ Ask many dragons to rush into it.

~ See them diving into the lower energies and gobbling them up.

~ Then see them delving deep into the land to clear energy stuck in the earth.

~ Ask angels to place their golden wings round the people there.

~ Ask unicorns to pour pure white Source love over the area.

~ See everything and everyone there cocooned in angelic light.

~ Know that your compassion has made a difference.

~ Remember to thank the angels, dragons and unicorns.

CHAPTER 5

Attuning to Unicorns

Unicorns connect with you the moment you think of them. And they constantly encourage you to purify your energies so that the link becomes clearer and stronger. Already millions of people are on their ascension path and are radiating beautiful light so that unicorns can work through them.

When you are attuned to unicorns, they illuminate the right ascension pathway for you. Then they light up your aura every time you call them in during meditation or talk about them or do a visualization with them. They touch your energy fields or your spiritual centres, usually your heart or third eye chakras, with their horn of light.

You may rarely realize just how much unicorns are assisting you. Nor may you be aware how much the ascension work you have already done on yourself has enabled unicorn energy to flood the planet.

Here is an example of how the unicorns move your destiny forward once they have connected with you. Franziska Siragusa is one of the principal teachers of the Diana Cooper School of

White Light. The first unicorn she saw looked like an elderly white horse who was a bit stocky and not very tall. He had a horn of light and was called Ezeriah. When he appeared, she felt very excited and joyful. Unicorns make things happen, and when, a few days later, the owner of a spiritual centre asked her to do a workshop about unicorns, she knew that Ezeriah was behind the invitation. She accepted, though at that time she was quite an introvert, not a good talker and very scared about running a workshop! She had no experience of teaching, but she recognized it was a golden opportunity. She knew she just had to do it, and indeed she did, and it set her on a wonderful new path as a spiritual teacher. It was a typical example of unicorns seeing a person's light of service, nudging them and giving them the qualities they needed to walk their life path.

Quite recently, when Franziska was teaching a course on Lemurian healing, Ezeriah appeared in a much more ethereal form. He looked younger than before and had more grace. What struck her most were his eyes, which were very clear and bright.

When she was teaching about Atlantis, one of the students, who was clairvoyant, said that he could see a very big unicorn with her. He looked much bigger than a usual horse and was called Simsa. This unicorn was helping Franziska to step into her power and supporting her while she was facilitating the course. She said it was transformative for her and for those who attended. There was incredible excitement and joy, much laughter and wonderful bonding in the group. Franziska was also amazed to learn that she could have more than one unicorn guide.

And then Sarah appeared. She called herself a ninth-dimensional diamond unicorn and appeared with diamonds in her beautiful mane. She explained that diamond unicorns worked with those wonderful gems to bring purity to the world. Franziska described her as very beautiful and graceful. She was pure love. Franziska said that her energy was quite different from that of the other two unicorns, as she was a much higher frequency and a female unicorn. Franziska felt that meeting her was a very important event in her life, for Sarah encouraged her to write a book about unicorns and gave her information for it. So, once they had connected with her, her unicorns continued to push Franziska along her path.

Everything is changing now for us all. Unicorns have sent in such a huge wave of their light that their images are everywhere. Children love them. People talk about them. Few realize that unicorns are real beings who answer prayers and can make a difference to people's lives. But the wave is getting stronger.

Unicorns are real beings
who answer prayers.

I was pondering this one day when I was walking the dogs. As I passed a mother and her child, the mother bent down to pick up the child's toy and said, 'You've dropped your unicorn.' I immediately saw a flash of white light – a unicorn was with them. For an instant it lit them up and I realized why unicorns had chosen to make their presence felt through a wave of toys and merchandizing. Each time someone notices a unicorn toy or image, unicorns can reach them, and in this way they are literally touching millions of people each day. No wonder the frequency everywhere is rising.

Unicorns are touching people
in all walks of life.

If you are a school teacher who is truly dedicated to inspiring children and passing information on to them, your intention will be reflected in the light you radiate. A unicorn will approach you and ignite your spiritual centres, filling them with the keys and codes that will enable you to influence your charges in a way that will enable them to integrate the information.

If you are a student with a desire to learn so that you can fulfil your soul mission, this will be mirrored in your energy fields. Again a unicorn will pour light into you so that you can absorb what you need. The unicorn will also give you determination and strength to fortify you.

Perhaps you are an honest politician with a vision for the betterment of the people you serve. Unicorn energy will support you and add the charisma and strength that you require.

You may be a lawyer or a business person with integrity, whose energy is in tune with the paradigm for the new Golden Age. If so, you can expect a nudge of assistance from the unicorn realm.

Doctors and nurses who have a pure commitment often attract the attention of unicorns. The more feminine energy the medic (or anyone else) carries, the easier it is for unicorns to connect with them. The Divine Feminine energies are empathy, love, dedication, wisdom, caring and a desire to heal and serve.

For most people, the most significant soul mission to which they will aspire in their lifetime is parenthood. Bringing a new soul into the world is considered to be incredibly important and a huge responsibility. In the current challenging climate, this role is often considered secondary to making money or even earning enough to live on. But when you earnestly want to serve the soul you have brought into incarnation, your unicorn will help you, if you ask. I was so delighted when a mother sent me a photograph of her baby with a unicorn Orb bathing it. Looking at it was a magical, joy-filled moment.

There are some people whose light shines so brightly that unicorns will gravitate to them automatically. Others will have to ask. But if they are ready to receive a unicorn's energy, their request will draw one to them. Then it will give them whatever qualities they need.

Sally Norden shared this beautiful story:

> *I met my unicorn, Stewy, around 10 years ago. He does have a long name beginning with 'S', but I couldn't pronounce it, so he said, 'You can call me Stewy.' He came to me during a meditation with my spirit guides and said, 'I can help you with anything you need. Just ask.'*
>
> *He usually comes galloping in! At first he had a beautiful golden horn, but it now seems to change colour depending on what colour I need. When I was with my ex, he would come in with hearts floating around his head, really happy for me. However, when something negative was about to happen, usually lies, his head would be bowed down, almost in warning.*
>
> *That is in the past now and I often call Stewy in. He gets me to put my hand on his horn and I get a burst of whatever it is he thinks I need. Lately his horn has been radiating full rainbow colours that are just wonderful. He has given me bursts of confidence, stamina and unconditional love. The energy he emits is very strong yet gentle. He is a fun-loving unicorn and I am so grateful to have met him.*
>
> *I work with children, and when they ask, I say I have my own unicorn called Stewy. When they say, 'Is he real?' I reply, 'Well, I can see him.'*

'Can he walk in here now?'

'He could if I asked him.'

'Would I be able to see him like I can see you now?'

'Let's try, shall we?'

As yet, no one else has seen him, but I know he is there and he is beautiful. That is all that counts.

YOUR UNICORN VISION

~ Sit quietly and come up with a vision to help others.

~ Focus on the aspects of it that will bring love, empowerment, hope or some other benefit to someone.

~ Sense that vision becoming a ball of white light.

~ Let it become bigger and brighter.

~ Mentally place that ball on the crown of your head and let it blaze out.

~ See or sense a unicorn being attracted to the light over you.

~ Feel yourself being lit up by the unicorn energy.

~ Pause as you absorb the qualities that are being downloaded into you.

~ Thank the unicorn.

Attuning to Your Personal Unicorn

As you read this book, you will connect more and more closely to your personal unicorn. However, to accelerate this process, here is an I AM attunement that you can use to link to its energy. An I AM attunement or decree affirms that your Monad, your original divine spark from God, aligns and merges in total harmony with whatever or whoever you are naming. In this case, it enables you to fuse with your unicorn energetically at the highest possible frequency and allows their gracious qualities and healing power to flow through you so that you can pass them on to others. You can place them into crystals or energize water with them or use them in any other way that feels right.

ATTUNING TO YOUR UNICORN

~ Find a place where you can be quiet and undisturbed.

~ Make sure you are very comfortable.

~ Unicorns particularly work with the third eye and heart chakras, so a special breath energizes your connection. Breathe comfortably into your heart centre and out of your third eye chakra.

~ Sense your heart becoming warmer with each in-breath.

~ Be aware of your third eye opening more and more with each out-breath, until you can see or sense a horn of enlightenment spiralling from your forehead.

~ Continue for as long as feels right.

~ When you are ready, visualize a ball of white light around you. This will connect you to the unicorn frequency.

~ With each out-breath, feel the ball filling with sparkling diamond-white light. Take your time.

~ On each in-breath, pure white energy fills your heart.

~ When your heart feels full, turn your attention to your hands.

~ Now on each out-breath the light flows from your heart down into your palm chakras, so that they open wider. Do this several times.

~ Now state silently or aloud: 'In the light of Source, I ask unicorns to pour their glorious light into and through me. From this moment I AM attuned to the unicorn realms. It is done.'

~ Feel or sense the light flooding into you and relax in this glorious energy for as long as you wish.

CHAPTER 6

Signs from Unicorns

Unicorns can remind you of their presence in many ways. If you are thinking about them and suddenly you see a beautiful rainbow, know that a being of light is near you. Or if you see a star that seems to be twinkling at you from the night sky, take a moment to feel the energy.

Dylan is the director of the unicorn documentary we are making. Not surprisingly, unicorns weren't exactly a part of his life until he met me and started hearing about them. Nevertheless, he was fascinated and read my last book on unicorns. On the morning before he sent me the contract for the documentary promo, he took his dog for a walk. When he put the dog bag in the bin, there was a toy unicorn peeping out of it! He ran into his house, saying, 'It's a sign! It's got to be a sign!'

That evening he took the contract to the post. On the way he passed a group of three people. A young woman was saying, 'I can't wait to wear my unicorn horn tonight!'

Just like angels, unicorns also leave little white feathers to tell you that they are near.

Asia Golden e-mailed to tell me that after she'd read my first book about unicorns many years earlier, she'd desperately wanted to meet unicorns or receive a sign from them. She did one of the meditations in the book and met a Pegasus. She wrote:

> *I really wanted something physical to 'know' they were there – like the white feathers. For days I prayed for a sign of their presence, to no avail. But I kept visualizing white feathers and being in the presence of the unicorn realm.*

Eventually Asia decided to give up and told herself that unicorns just weren't with her. At that point she went out into her garden. She wrote:

> *Literally there was a gigantic – and I mean gigantic – pile of white feathers by my meditation hut – out of nowhere, and it definitely wasn't from dead birds. I was so giddy! I still feel my heart chakra open when I think of that day many years ago, as it was a very dark time in my life and unicorns lifted me up and made me feel special and safe! And they still send me white feathers when I am feeling doubt or fear and let me know that magic is all around.*

Some responses are unmistakable. Janis Moody wrote to tell me what happened when she went on a unicorn walk. This is a walk when you affirm you have merged with unicorns and are seeing everything from a higher perspective through their eyes of love. Wherever you go on your walk, you act as if you are a unicorn and bless people and places with their energy. It is a very special and sacred thing to do. Janis explained that in Oklahoma at that time there had been massive rains and record flooding. To avoid this, she was guided to take a different route from her usual one. And there in the middle of the street lay a sweet little china unicorn. It was covered in mud, so Janis took it home, cleaned it up and placed it among her crystals. She felt it was wonderful confirmation that unicorns were present. She sent me a photograph of it with her crystals and indeed it was beautiful.

The greatest validation you can have of the presence of unicorns is your own response to them. I love this story that Alicia Saa sent me:

> *I had shared some stories about unicorns with my online community. The next day I received a message from the mother of a Down's syndrome boy. The child loved unicorns, but his father didn't feel comfortable about it and every time his son talked about unicorns, he said to him, 'Unicorns are for girls, not for boys.'*
>
> *When the mother saw the information that I was sharing about unicorns, she understood why the boy liked them so much. Her heart felt lighter and more vibrant than ever before, and when her husband arrived home she told him everything about the angelic realms and these magnificent light beings.*
>
> *To her surprise, suddenly he began to cry. He went to his son's room and told him how special he was. He also told him that angels had changed his mind about unicorns. The next day he took his son to buy a unicorn soft toy and from that moment on he totally believed in them.*
>
> *The father's own reaction was his proof. This story made my heart burst with hope!*

Alicia also shared the following story:

One day I was planning to take my younger son to the movies. However, when we were ready to go, the car wouldn't start. I said to my son that this was happening for the highest good and then I called the American Automobile Association, who came within the hour and changed the car battery. At last we were ready to go out and then the magic happened: we saw a balloon in the street! We stopped, and my son got out of the car to pick it up. It said, 'Believe in unicorns.'

She sent me a photo of it!

Fiona Sutton also sent me a photograph, and when I looked at it, I could hardly believe my eyes. Here is her story:

We were walking by the beautiful lily ponds at Bosherston, in Pembrokeshire in west Wales, when I could really sense unicorn energy, so mentally I asked them to reveal themselves – ideally in one of my photos. Many pictures later, we stopped for lunch at a pub. By then I'd completely forgotten about my request, so as I was looking through my pictures I wasn't consciously looking for anything. But as I did so, one of the pictures just seemed to jump out at me. The light in the middle of the lake seemed strange, and even though the image was small, there appeared to be a clear outline of a unicorn head.

Zooming in, I was just amazed. I could see two unicorns. The head and neck of one were very clear indeed, and there was no mistaking the eye, nostril and muzzle. There was only a partial view of the unicorn to his left, but there was no mistaking the horn. The more I looked at them, the clearer they became and the more detail I could take in. I was struck by the number three I could see on the unicorn's neck, as I knew this to be a very sacred number, being representative of the Holy Trinity. I was also struck by the cross inside the green halo around his head, and Googling this, discovered it was a cruciform halo, something I had never heard of before. I was surprised to discover that this is also representative of Christ consciousness. And I know from reading your wonderful book The Wonder of Unicorns *that the unicorn itself is symbolic of Christ consciousness. How amazingly synchronistic!*

I looked at the photograph. The two unicorns were plainly reflected in the lake, but at first I could not see the number three on the neck of one of them. Then it jumped out at me as clear as a bell. The cross surrounded by a halo was unmissable too. And needless to say, a clear reflection of not one but two unicorns in a pond is highly unusual!

In the e-mail to which she attached the photograph, Fiona added:

I feel truly blessed to have captured this photo. It is particularly meaningful to me, as just four days before taking it, two unicorns had appeared to me in a meditation and I had written about them in a journal. I had described one as very graceful and light and the other as heavy and majestic; weirdly, just as they appeared in the photo. But even more meaningfully, since starting to walk my spiritual path, I've found two unicorns have been leading the way, appearing through cards, dreams and even in the form of a statue from a departed friend.

Unicorns really are magic. Reading Fiona's message and looking at her photograph reminded me to look much more carefully at the pictures I take.

I was also sent a magnificent series of photographs by Hara, who has a huge white unicorn head above her bed. She wrote:

One day I was feeling sad, so I sat in my bedroom to meditate. I asked, 'Is there really something beyond the physical, beyond our imagination...? Is there a God? Or are we making it all up? Are there angels? Angels, are you there? Are you here? Do you hear me? Can you help me? Can you show me something...?' I wanted answers. I wanted proof. I wanted contact or a connection. Something. I was desperate.

I said, 'If there is something out there, then show me! Show me something! Something that I can see! I am a physical human being and I want to see something physical! I want physical proof that you – whoever that is – exist!'

I was screaming inside like a little girl and it was almost funny. And then the energy in the room started to change. It became electrified and light and joyous and I heard a voice saying, 'Okay, now you can open your eyes...' And I did. And what I saw was one of the most beautiful things I have seen in my whole life! What I saw when I opened my eyes was a brilliant, gorgeous, magical rainbow on the unicorn head and a big pale pink haze around it. It was a real rainbow! But there had been no rain and there was no sun hitting that room. It was a cloudy grey day. And yet the colours were so intense. I'd never seen such brilliant colours. What I was witnessing was so amazing that after a few minutes of being totally speechless, I found my eyes filling up so much that I couldn't see anymore. I was so emotional, so ecstatic, so amazed, so happy that I was shaking! For a couple of minutes, I was just looking at this incredible view and muttering to myself, 'How could they do something so beautiful and so personal and perfect and magic?'

A few minutes later the rainbow was still there, and as soon as I'd wiped my eyes I asked the unicorns if they would allow me to take a picture of it, because I never ever wanted to forget it. They agreed, so I ran, grabbed my camera and got a few pictures! After that, the rainbow slowly disappeared and left me with undeniable and endless faith, trust, love, happiness and joy. And then I said to myself, 'Whatever happens in life, I believe!'

Indeed, the photographs of the unicorn head lit up by a brilliant rainbow were breathtaking. I gasped when I saw them. The spiritual realms have endless ways of giving us proof.

Kerstin Joost is a medical doctor and a Master Teacher in the Diana Cooper School of White Light. When she first moved to Zurich, she did not know the city, so she wandered randomly and asked her unicorn to direct her. Finding herself in front of a museum advertising an exhibition on Buddhism, she entered and was guided to the last room. To her amazement, inside it was a magnificent golden unicorn. She had never seen a unicorn in Buddhism before and she knew her guide had taken her to see it. On the way home she asked her unicorn to tell her its name. She had asked before, but never received an answer. This time, when she reached her apartment, the phone rang and it was a man calling for medical advice. He said very clearly, 'My name is Lucas and you write it with a "c" – Lucas.' She knew instantly that this was her unicorn's name.

Marilou also received a unicorn message. She and her husband were on vacation at an apartment hotel in southern Spain. They had been there for almost two weeks when one morning at breakfast her husband took a knife out of the cutlery drawer that had a unicorn stamped on the blade. They hadn't seen it before and it was the only one like that. Beside the unicorn were etched the words 'Kom Kom', which they interpreted as a summons! So they decided to watch one of my Unicorn Zooms and connect more to unicorns!

CHAPTER 7

Unicorn Colours

I am sometimes asked, 'What does it mean if you see or have an impression of a coloured unicorn? Is this possible or is it an illusion?'

This is an interesting question, because all images are valid and come to give you information. However, some are from the higher spiritual realms and others may arise from your unconscious processes.

The Colours of Unicorns

Unicorns radiate purity. That is their essence. White contains all colours and these illumined beings usually show themselves in this radiance. However, a unicorn may choose to reveal one particular aspect of its divinity to you, so may appear to be a particular colour. If that colour is pastel, clear and has a pure quality about it, accept it as a message from the unicorn realms. If it is murky, dingy, lurid or opaque, the image probably comes from your personal unconscious and is asking to be explored.

Occasionally people report that a black unicorn has come to them. We sometimes associate a black horse with greed, power and control over others, but a rare black unicorn represents mystery, magic and transformation. If a black unicorn comes to you, ask yourself how it feels before you accept it. It may have come to nurture an idea or bring forward your wisdom.

The arrival of a pale pink unicorn indicates that it is touching you with pure transcendent love.

A light-blue-hued one brings the gift of higher communication and invites you to ensure that your words and thoughts are of the highest integrity.

A soft-green-tinted unicorn is bringing you balance and harmony. It is asking you actively to seek peace and contentment.

If the unicorn carries the palest translucent yellow or gold, it is reminding you to bring your knowledge and wisdom forward or suggesting that it is about to download more into you.

Peach is a mixture of the pink of love and the gold of wisdom. A unicorn bearing this shade is showering you with wondrous love and wisdom, so relax and accept it.

Two other very spiritual hues occasionally proffered by these beings of light are light lilac or mauve. The lilac contains more of the blue of healing or communication, while the mauve holds more of the pink of love. Both of these colours call on you to act in a purely spiritual way.

Sometimes participants in seminars have met a rainbow-coloured unicorn. Rainbows symbolize hope and the opening of new possibilities. They always promise joy.

The Colours of Unicorns' Eyes

I used to see or sense unicorns' eyes as light blue and assumed that other people sensed the same. Then one day during an online seminar when I was taking participants into a meditation to meet their unicorn, I was guided to ask them to look into its eyes. That's when I learned otherwise. I was intrigued and excited to discover the variety and intensity of colours and colour combinations that people reported. One lady shared that her unicorn had deep-violet eyes; another, soft pink with shimmering gold rims. A man described many colours swirling together and sparkling with stars. He said it was 'like looking into galaxies'. A striking combination was deep amber, black and blue, giving the impression of great power.

My guide, Kumeka, tells me that a unicorn's eyes are normally light blue. However, unicorns are great teachers and they sometimes take the opportunity to mirror back to you aspects of your own soul energy that you might not be aware of.

So, the person who saw deep violet that day was being reminded that at a soul level she was very spiritual and could transmute the lower frequencies of others. The lady who saw soft pink with shimmering gold rims understood that she carried much love and wisdom in her soul. The man who described looking into galaxies recalled his dreams of travelling to the stars and wanted to explore the path of intergalactic mastery. The woman who was shown deep amber, black and blue and felt this was very powerful was put in touch with the power of her soul.

Here is a very simple exercise to find the colours of your own soul.

FINDING THE COLOURS OF YOUR SOUL

For this exercise you need paper and a selection of crayons or felt pens. You also need trust and intuition!

~ Find a place where you can be quiet and undisturbed.

~ Light a candle, a white one if possible, to raise the energy.

~ Draw the outline of an eye on the paper. If you want to, you can add the black pupil in the centre and eyelashes at the edges.

~ Close your eyes and mentally ask unicorns to guide you to find the colours of your soul.

~ Decide how many colours you need. Let the number drop into your mind.

~ With your eyes still closed, reach out and let the unicorns guide you to the right colours.

~ Half open your eyes and colour in your eye with your soul colours.

~ When you have finished, fully open your eyes and consider what you have created. Is this what you expected? Have you learned anything about your soul?

~ Thank the unicorns.

What do the colours mean?

The Colours of Your Soul

• White indicates a pure soul.

• Silver indicates that you have magical gifts.

• Gold indicates a wise soul.

• Platinum indicates a soul who is very disciplined and has potential.

- Pink indicates a loving soul.

- Pale yellow indicates a soul who is a teacher, philosopher or thinker.

- Orange indicates a happy soul.

- Red indicates a vibrant soul with leadership qualities.

- Pale blue indicates a soul who is a healer.

- Pale turquoise indicates a soul who communicates clearly.

- Deep blue indicates a soul who communicates with wisdom and integrity.

- Light green indicates a soul who is balanced and loves nature.

- Violet indicates a very spiritual soul.

- Rainbow indicates a soul who spreads light and hope.

The Colours of Unicorns' Horns

Unicorns develop spiritually through service. The purer the light spiralling from their third eye, the more enlightened they are. Sometimes a unicorn is depicted with a white, silver or rainbow horn; at others with a golden one, indicating great wisdom. The more they evolve, the deeper the gold. Recently, highly evolved unicorns with platinum or rainbow-coloured horns have been entering the aura of Earth. They carry transcendent joy and bliss. As for a diamond horn, that is awesome!

Unicorns are healers and teachers and they can take a ray from the spectrum of colours that make up white light if they want to give you a specific energy via their horn. The colours have a variety of meanings and the shades are all pastels. Use your intuition and interpret the colours for yourself, but here is a little guidance:

- White suggests purity.

- Silver infers that the unicorns are bringing you magic and good fortune.

- Gold offers wisdom.

- Platinum implies higher possibilities.

- Pink embraces you with love.

- Pale yellow carries universal information.

- Pale blue enfolds you in healing.

- Pale turquoise proposes clear communication.

- Light green advises you to come into balance.

- Rainbow inspires you with hope.

If you want to discover which colour your unicorn is radiating from its third eye for you today and to see the colours of your own soul reflected in its eyes, here is a visualization for you:

EXPLORING THE COLOURS OF YOUR SOUL AND THE COLOUR OF YOUR UNICORN'S HORN

~ Find a place where you can be quiet and undisturbed.

~ Light a candle, a white one if possible, to raise the energy.

~ Close your eyes and relax.

~ Imagine you are in a beautiful, peaceful valley filled with grass and flowers. Birds are singing.

~ A magnificent waterfall is pouring down one side of the valley.

~ As you approach it, you realize it is a cascade of pure white light.

~ You step into it and it flows over you, cleansing you.

~ You sense the light flowing through your head and round your brain, down through your neck and shoulders and arms, down through your heart, down through your solar plexus and internal organs, and down into your hips and thighs and legs. As it pours through you, you are being purified.

~ You step out into the beautiful valley and a shimmering white unicorn is standing quietly waiting for you, ready to give you information about your soul energy.

~ Notice the colours in its horn of light.

~ As it approaches you, it sends a sparkling shower of light over you, then lowers its head in a friendly greeting.

~ You look into its eyes. What colour or colours are they? What do they reflect to you? Is there a message there for you?

~ Stand for a moment in your unicorn's glorious aura.

~ Thank your unicorn and watch it disappear into the distance.

Chapter 8

Unicorns and Children

U nicorns have a special connection with children, especially babies, who still carry the pure essence of Source energy. This creates a natural attraction for unicorns.

Babies still see spiritual beings and you can watch them laugh as their eyes follow some distant light. This is often a loved one in spirit or an angel or unicorn.

Lots of children now ask for unicorn parties. I remember one little girl who had absolutely set her heart on one. There was to be a unicorn cake, unicorn hats and even unicorn games. I felt that this was going to be a specially blessed birthday, and when I saw her the following day, she was beaming. She said it had been the best party she'd ever had. Of course it had been, because unicorns had been there, honouring her birthday and raising the frequency.

Birthdays are such special times. Lady Gaia, the angel who overlights Earth, gives us a personal invitation to our incarnation and we choose our day of birth very carefully so we can catch the right cosmic current to step onto our destined path. On the anniversary of that day each year, angels sing over us. If we are connected to unicorns, they shower a gracious blessing over us too.

Many of the children being born now are enlightened ones who have been specially prepared to take our planet into the new Golden Age. Unicorns have connected with these souls before they have incarnated and have been present at their birth. No wonder unicorn birthday parties are so special for them.

Children See Unicorns

Susana is from Portugal, but lives in England with her partner and two boys. She e-mailed me a wonderful story:

> *In September 2013 we moved from Felixstowe to Salisbury. One day not long after we'd moved, my son, who was then four years old, was looking up at the sky as if he was looking for something. I asked what the matter was and he replied, 'Mummy, I can't see those horses that have wings and a horn in their forehead.' I asked what he meant by that. His reply was, 'Mummy, when we were in Felixstowe, there were lots of flying horses, but I can't see them here. I miss them.'*
>
> *I had never talked with him about unicorns and I was really surprised that he knew what they were, because at that time we didn't see them in the shops as we do today. I'd always thought they were children's fantasies, but after what he told me, I started to believe that they were real.*
>
> *My son is now eight. He was five when his brother was born and he said, 'Mum, do you know that the baby is able to see angels and fairies? I can't see them anymore. I miss them.'*

I asked Susana for permission to use her son's story. She spoke to him and he said that I could use his name too. His name is Alexandre Alves. What a special and gifted child.

A few months after Susana wrote to me, I spoke to her and Alexandre online and was very impressed by Alexandre, who shone with light. He couldn't remember the unicorns, but recalled seeing angels. His mother told me some incredible stories about him.

One day when he was five years old, he asked, 'Do you remember when I chose you, Mum? I chose you. You chose Dad, and Dad didn't choose anyone.'

Another time he was crying because his mother was going to die before him. She comforted him by saying that they would always be together. The following day in the supermarket he piped up, 'Mum, you lied to me. This is our last life together, because at the end of this life I am going up a level.'

One night before going to bed he announced out of the blue, 'Mum, do you know that you have a baby waiting for you? He's going to be born here in England, but he needs to have a Portuguese name. His name is Chico!' This is short for Francisco, which apparently was a name they had never mentioned. No one in the family was called that and at that time the only Portuguese words Alexandre knew had been taught him by his parents. Yet he knew the Portuguese name of his yet-to-be-conceived brother. And two years later, Francisco was born.

Susana shared other stories that Alexandre had told her about his past lives and otherworldly experiences. No wonder I could sense unicorns around him.

Children Are Helped by Unicorns

Unicorns love the innocence of children, especially those who are trying to help themselves. If you know a child who is being tormented or is unhappy in any way, ask unicorns to help, for magic can happen.

Lorena del Cueto from Argentina told me that her youngest daughter, Meli, was having a difficult time at school because she was being bullied. They had talked to the teachers at the school, but they didn't know what to do about it and were unhelpful, so Meli realized that she would have to do something herself. She decided that she would treat every day as if it was a new start. Her parents helped her to be stronger and strengthened themselves at the same time.

Then the child had another difficult day with a friend at school. She cried a lot and Lorena talked to the other girl's parents to try to resolve the problem.

That night Meli had a dream: 'Mum, I had a wonderful dream! A beautiful white unicorn came to me and I got on it and we flew together, saving the world. Then we came back and we hugged and then the unicorn left.'

Meli was really happy and Lorena was happy for her! She was sure that her daughter was being protected and that everything was going to turn out fine for her. She wrote, 'It was a beautiful blessing that such a pure energy contacted a child that really needed it. It was so beautiful! So miraculous! And a wonderful message from heaven!' She started to research unicorn energy and talked to Meli about it. The child was really happy and full of hope, which made a real difference to her life at school.

Lorena added, 'Meli's dream happened before there were unicorns everywhere on T-shirts, sweatshirts, folders, pencil cases, sheets, pillows, cups, glasses, etc.'

When a unicorn comes to you in a dream, it touches you at a soul level and changes your life.

Unicorn Blessings

I was asked to visit a severely disabled girl in a wheelchair. She was in touch with angels and had recently seen a unicorn. Although she could not talk, she could communicate by indicating letters or pictures on a screen. She must have developed incredible patience to convey her thoughts and needs in this way. By this means we conversed for hours and I realized what a special soul she was. I was deeply touched when she expressed that her greatest desire was to serve others. I explained to her about unicorn blessings and she was delighted, as she realized sending unicorn blessings was something she could do to help others. She literally radiated joy. I left feeling humbled yet elevated.

So, what is a unicorn blessing? A blessing is an act of grace in which you send another person heartfelt love, light and the qualities that they need. In a unicorn blessing, you call in unicorns and ask them to touch the person with whatever energy they need. For example, if you were to see a very sad person, you would call in unicorns and ask them to bless the person with happiness. Then you would envision them being happy. If you saw a homeless person, you would ask the unicorns to help them, under grace, to find the perfect home. If you met a lonely person, you would ask the unicorns to touch their heart and bless them with friendships.

I have literally seen and sensed pure white light shooting across the world to touch someone when I have called in a unicorn blessing for them.

Here is a unicorn visualization to help children. You can do it for your own child, a child you know, or hundreds of children.

If you have a child, you can even ask them to join you on the journey.

Helping Children

~ Find a place where you can be quiet and undisturbed.

~ Place your feet on the floor if you can and picture your silver Earth Star chakra below your feet grounding you firmly.

~ Focus on your breathing until you sense yourself relax.

~ Then imagine yourself sitting on the white shores of a beautiful tranquil lake on a balmy evening.

~ With you is the child or children you are focusing on, all expectantly watching a beautiful moon rising.

~ Out of the night sky you see wondrous shimmering white unicorns appearing, one for every child and one for you.

~ You all happily greet your unicorn and find yourself on its back, feeling safe yet full of anticipation.

~ Each child mentally explains what they want to their unicorn. You hold the energy as this happens.

~ The unicorns fly away, taking everyone through the stars to a beautiful plateau surrounded by mountains.

~ Here everything is happy and peaceful.

~ The children get off their unicorns, who lead them to a garden of deep-blue flowers. From their horns, they pour deep-blue light over their charges, forming a protective cloak over them. Notice how confident and safe the children now seem.

~ And then they move to a pink garden, where the unicorns touch the children's hearts with love. See their eyes become full of love and trust.

~ Finally they move to an orange garden, where the unicorns bathe the children in wonderful happy orange light. See them laughing and joyful.

~ At last the children climb onto their unicorns again.

~ They fall asleep on the unicorns' backs as they glide smoothly, gently and peacefully through the universe.

~ It is while they sleep that unicorn magic happens to them.

~ And they wake as the unicorns drift back over the lake and land softly on the white sand.

~ The children dismount and thank the unicorns, then wave goodbye to them.

~ Open your eyes, knowing that something magical has happened to help the children.

Connecting Children with Unicorns

Every time you talk about unicorns you are bringing them closer to you and your children. But there are many other ways in which children can connect with them.

Crystal Grids

One day I was playing with two of my grandchildren whom I don't see very often, as they live some distance away. The two little girls asked me to make crystal grids with them, so naturally

I was delighted. They love crystals and happily spend ages in crystal shops, often choosing crystals to give as presents.

That day I asked them what they wanted to make the crystal grids for, and Taliya, who was then seven, immediately announced that she wanted to make a grid that would help her be closer to her unicorn! She set off round the house and garden to search for white crystals and pebbles and a coloured cloth on which to lay them out. She also produced a little unicorn pendant and a white feather. Then she spent a happy time making a spiral-shaped grid to enable her to have a closer connection with her unicorn.

I saw her again a couple of months later and asked her if it had helped her know her unicorn better. She assured me that it had.

I share more on crystal grids later on in the book.

Patterns in the Sand

It seems to me that children of any age, even teenagers, enjoy making patterns on the beach with pebbles. These patterns are in fact grids. You might like to suggest that the children ask unicorns to energize the shapes by pouring their light over them. They can imagine a column of light going up from the grid to the heavens. Then they can call in blessings or qualities for themselves or send them to other people.

You can make patterns on the lawn or anywhere. While white pebbles or crystals are perfect, you can also use fir cones or anything natural. Intention is the most important element in making a grid.

A Selenite Wand

Katie, who is a medical professional, certainly doesn't talk about unicorns to many people other than her young children, who each know their own very well. Her little girl rides on her unicorn most nights. Her son says his selenite wand is his connection to unicorns and sleeps with it under his pillow.

If your child wants to connect to unicorns, why not get them a selenite wand to sleep with? They really are magic wands and many children love to use them to touch trees, flowers, animals, insects and even people and make beautiful wishes for them.

Unicorn Tag

In this game, one child is the unicorn and has to try to catch another child. When it does so, it holds out its hands to give the child it has caught a unicorn blessing or wish.

MAKING A UNICORN STABLE

Place a tablecloth, preferably a white one, over a table. Underneath is your stable. Here the child or children can look after their unicorns.

What can they do with them? Here are a few suggestions:

~ Call the unicorns in.

~ Feed, water and groom them.

~ Name them.

~ Draw and decorate a name plate for each of them.

~ Talk to them and listen to what they have to say.

This may be seem to be a game, but it is a very good way for children to connect with and learn about unicorns. All the time they are engaged in this, their celestial guardian will be with them.

MAKING A UNICORN GARDEN

If you have a small piece of garden to spare, you and your child may like to turn it into a unicorn garden.

The most important thing when creating this is your intention. It is an offering to your unicorns, so first clear the space to make it neat and tidy!

What then? Here are a few suggestions:

~   Collect some big stones or small rocks. It is fun and effective when you paint these white.

~   Gather anything from nature. If you like painting, collect twigs, paint them white and plant them. You can do the same with fir cones.

~   Unicorns love shimmer, so sprinkle some glitter!

~   Find a bowl and sink it into the soil, then fill it with water.

~   Plant some flowers.

~   Add ornaments, toys or anything else that feels right.

Enjoy your garden and ask unicorns to join you there.

Making a Miniature Unicorn Garden on a Plate or in a Bowl

The same principles apply as when you are making a garden on a piece of land. The most important thing is your intention. So, find a clean plate or bowl in which to make your miniature garden. Then you might like to:

~   Place some moss or oasis or other material on the plate as a foundation for your garden.

~   Collect pebbles, crystals or stones. Think of a quality, then hold a pebble and ask your unicorn to bless it with that quality.

~   Carefully place the stones in your garden. You may like to use them to make a path.

~   Find a small bowl and fill it with water or use a pocket mirror to represent a pond.

~   Place small flowers or leaves in the garden (remember to ask them before you pick them).

~   Add tiny model people or animals – anything that brings the garden to life.

~   When you are pleased with your miniature garden, invite unicorns into it.

Making Your Own Unicorn Cards

~   Find some thick paper, if possible. If you can't find stiff paper, just use ordinary paper.

~   Cut it into small squares.

~ Draw a unicorn on each one. It doesn't have to be a work of art – a stick unicorn will do.

~ Then think of a message or a quality, such as happiness or mercy, and write this on the card.

~ Ask unicorns to touch the cards with their light.

~ Give the cards to people with love. You are blessing the recipients with unicorn energy.

WISHING ON A UNICORN CRYSTAL

Crystals hold energy and intention and children love them.

~ Find a clear quartz or selenite crystal.

~ Hold it lovingly in your hand and invoke unicorns.

~ Make your wish and ask the unicorns to grant it if it is for the highest good.

Please note you don't have to be or have a child to enjoy doing any of the above.

CHAPTER 9

Unicorns and Animals

Animals are right-brain orientated, so they have a clear mind and therefore a pure mental body. Because of this innocence, unicorns have a love and affinity for them.

Holly e-mailed me about some kittens who had been abandoned near a park:

> *I often checked on the kittens as I had grown very fond of them. Some were very friendly and enjoyed petting and attention. I didn't see one of them for two weeks and then a couple pointed out a long-haired tabby in obvious distress under a prickly bush. I immediately recognized the kitten and could tell she was ready to pass away. I had to make some arrangements, but returned to search for her after dark with my car headlights. The kitten was no longer under the prickly bush, but another volunteer found her nearby. I took her to a vet, who graciously accepted her and assisted her in passing over. I named her Grace and returned home, deeply saddened.*

As I woke the following morning, I had a vision of a unicorn pushing Grace out from under the prickly, painful sharp branches and over to the corner where we had discovered her. I believe a unicorn wanted me to know she had assisted me. It was amazing, because I had been able to retrieve Grace and pick her up easily without injuring myself or frightening her. I am very grateful for this unicorn's help and assistance.

I think Holly's story is absolutely amazing! Not only did the unicorn help the animal, but then gave Holly a vision of how it had assisted.

A few weeks later Holly e-mailed me again, this time to say that unicorns were showing up occasionally with the abandoned kittens that she fed. One was a black-and-white tuxedo kitten called Bingo. Unfortunately, he passed away and Holly was very sad about it. Later she saw her unicorn lift him from the place where he had died into the light. She believes Bingo received love and care from the unicorn after he passed.

Holly also tried to rescue a large orange-and-white Maine Coon cat called Kaylin, who decided to break out of her cage and make a run for it. Unfortunately Holly couldn't locate her, but her unicorn came to her, smiling, and showed her Kaylin running into the light. She knew then that everything was all right.

However clear our impressions, and even our knowing, it is always lovely to receive confirmation from another source. Holly explained that a dear friend of hers who had passed away several years before had also been deeply committed to cats and she had seen him waving happily at her from spirit and confirming what the unicorn had showed her.

Animals originate from many different stars and planets and have a link with souls who originate from the same planet or star system as they do. In the Golden Era of Atlantis it was considered perfectly natural to see cats and rabbits communing together, for example, for they both came from Orion.

Horses and unicorns from Sirius have a special bond, so you may see an ethereal white horse galloping among its friends. In addition, those who love and care for horses are linked to unicorn energy.

As many people know, my dog, Venus, is a 'character' dog. She is a Papajack – Papillon mixed with Jack Russell. She is a pretty little fluffy white dog, but her heart and soul are terrier. She is loyal, intelligent, joyful and totally adorable. To me, she is five kilos of pure love and joy. On the downside, she sometimes jerks the extending lead from my hand and races off, trailing it behind her. It then becomes inextricably tangled in a thicket and I spend too much of my time plunging through brambles and nettles to rescue her.

She is in fact clearly devoted to helping me to develop patience, for I often have to wait for her to return from a hunting expedition, tail wagging, very pleased with herself and totally unrepentant. I have learned the hard way that when people tell me their gardens are totally dog-proof, this doesn't necessarily mean that they are Venus-proof. She can flatten herself like a mouse or squeeze through a miniscule hole. Every time she disappears, I call on Archangel Fhelyai, the angel of animals, to look after her and bring her back safely, if it is for the highest good. Then I relax and trust that she is being looked after. Though I sometimes feel I am asking too much too often of Archangel Fhelyai!

One day, as I was waiting tolerantly for Venus to reappear, as terrier owners so often do, I had an image of a unicorn chasing her back to me. Sure enough, seconds later the miscreant raced into view! The next day, when she inevitably vanished again, I called on Archangel Fhelyai to look after her. Then a little while later I asked a unicorn to push her in my direction. She appeared as if by magic! Now I call on unicorns whenever I think she has been gone too long! I am constantly learning new ways in which these magnificent beings can help us.

Unicorns love the peace and stillness of nature. One morning as I was walking my dogs in a quiet place by a little stream, I was visualizing Ascension Flames bringing their energy down through the trees into the earth. Then I stopped to listen to a sad oak tree that was feeling overburdened because there were now so few oak trees to share their work. Suddenly my little Venus barked to draw my attention to a pure white squirrel on a branch above me! It was gorgeous and I was enchanted. I watched it until it leapt out of sight. Seeing a white squirrel felt like a reward and I was sure it had come from unicorns.

All animals appear to give us a message. Squirrels tell us that there is always a solution to a problem, so if we have a problem and can't solve it, we are to keep trying. The fact that I had seen a pure white squirrel that day meant: 'Look at the problem from a higher perspective and the answer will appear.' So when I reached home I sat quietly and asked unicorns to help me see everything from a higher, expanded viewpoint. Within moments, I had made the important new decision to move house.

Helping Animals

If you want to help animals, there are many ways you can ask unicorns to assist you. You may have a pet who needs some healing. Or a creature that you have an affinity with may be trying to do really important service work but be totally unappreciated by humans. Badgers immediately spring to mind, for they have been bringing balance to the world and trying to transmute the negativity within the earth for centuries without any acknowledgement of their efforts.

You can also ask unicorns to pour light onto a particular species, for instance endangered ones like gorillas, who need so much help.

ASKING UNICORNS TO HELP A PET

~ Find a place where you can be quiet and undisturbed.

~ Close your eyes, visualize a pet, yours or someone else's, and gently stroke it.

~ What does it need?

~ Invoke a unicorn and see or sense it arrive in a blaze of white fire.

~ Ask it to help the creature in whatever way is best.

~ Be aware of pure white light from the unicorn bathing the animal.

~ Thank the unicorn and trust that healing has taken place.

ASKING UNICORNS TO HELP AN ANIMAL IN NEED

~ Find a place where you can be quiet and undisturbed.

~ Know that no matter what animal comes to you, you are totally safe.

~ Close your eyes and call one to you or just allow one to appear in your inner view.

~ Gently tell it you are asking a unicorn to help it in whatever way is necessary.

~   Have a sense that the creature understands and is grateful.

~   Invoke a unicorn and be aware of it arriving in a shower of white sparkles.

~   The unicorn touches the animal with its horn of light and pours a cascade of diamond energy over and into it.

~   The unicorn or the animal may have a message for you, so take a moment to listen.

~   Thank the unicorn and trust that it has made a difference.

CHAPTER 10

Unicorns and the
Power of Numbers

There are many powerful pools of energy out in the universe, ready to help you if you call them in. The Mahatma energy, the Archangel Rays and the Ascension Flames are examples of these. In addition, at a cosmic level each number forms a pool of ninth-dimensional energy. In their true universal form, they all have a very powerful influence. By the time they have stepped their energy down to reach most of us, they have a considerably diluted impact. Nevertheless, even in a weak form their vibration can touch and affect us.

I have often talked about numbers over the years, though I am not a numerologist. It was only when I was writing this chapter with unicorns guiding me that I really and truly understood just how much numbers affect us.

With the advent of digital clocks and watches, numbers have become increasingly significant. Used with wisdom, they are a tool for higher spiritual understanding. Tuning in to them can accelerate your spiritual growth. However, when you add unicorn energy to the cosmic vibration of a number, the outcome is magnified and can be life-changing.

Life Path Numbers

At your pre-life consultation on the inner planes before your birth, your soul chooses the moment of your birth. This is of vital importance, for it sets you on your life path and after that you are subtly influenced by the number of your path. When your unicorn adds its light to that number, then takes you deeply into its vibration, it enhances its positive effect on your life.

Finding Your Life Path Number

You can discover the number that overlights your life path by adding the individual numbers in the day, month and year of your birth.

For example, 29 July 1970 is 2 + 9 + 7 + 1 + 9 + 7 + 0 = 35. Reduce it to a single digit by adding the 3 + 5 = 8. Anyone born on this day is under the influence of number 8.

The Vibration of Number One

The qualities of number one are independence, individualism, uniqueness, dynamism and ambition. If you are unconventional or have great ideas that you want to market, or you originate projects or instigate movements, this is your number. It enables you to bring focus and attention to your vision.

The other side of this number can be that you are so focused on your goal that you do not build a support system and may feel alone or isolated. Alternatively, you may become autocratic or bossy.

Number one helps you to be the number one, the boss, the leader, the decision-taker, the courageous one. You are the driver whose energy and force move everyone forward. It also indicates a new beginning is available to you. This is a masculine number.

When your unicorn adds its light to number one, it balances its masculine impact with feminine energy. This doesn't dilute its special qualities. However, it does soothe the excesses that one sometimes induces.

The Vibration of Number Two

The qualities of this number are co-operation, support, balance, sensitivity and partnership.

Under the influence of this number, you are a peacemaker who loves harmony, but you are also resilient and you can stand in your power. If you are diplomatic, tactful, discreet, peaceful and subtle, you could be a harmonious support, adviser or invaluable power behind the throne to someone more thrusting.

This is a feminine number that holds the soothing, loving, vulnerable, caring, creative, romantic energy of the Divine Feminine. However, too much sensitivity often means being easily hurt.

When your unicorn adds its light to number two, it enables you to find more peace and harmony in your life. It enhances creativity and artistic ability and raises the frequency of this number with joy and Source love. It increases your charisma.

The Vibration of Number Three

Three is the number of optimism, enthusiasm, expansion and motivation. If you inspire others and make people feel good, you vibrate with three. It is sometimes called the 'sunshine number', because those who resonate with it tend to be happy, relaxed and comfortable within themselves. This is the number of communication and the ability to express yourself openly and confidently.

The downside of this vibration is the capacity to be controlling, authoritarian or too scattered.

When your unicorn adds its light to number three, the vibration can enhance your creativity, artistic ability and communication skills. It can expand your life and bring you serendipity and joy.

The Vibration of Number Four

Four is the vibration of stability, practicality and dependability. If you wish to create a solid foundation and build upon it with honesty, in an orderly and methodical way, this is the number to call in. If your project needs you to be detailed, systematic and precise, focus on number four.

As with all numbers, there is a downside, though. Four is 'square'. It can be rigid, which means it likes habit and ritual. If you feel this is the case with you, make changes!

When your unicorn adds its light to number four, a very strong and stable base is formed. Everything that you could possibly need

*for solid, dependable success is available
to you, yet you can still be flexible.*

The Vibration of Number Five

Five has a dynamic vibration. It touches you with a desire for freedom and adventure and the courage to go for it. Bathe in this number if you wish to be a powerful promoter or persuasive salesperson. It will help you to be quick-thinking. If you like to experiment and explore and are so easily irked by the mundane that you have several projects on the go, you are being influenced by this number.

The downside of this number is a desire for immediate results and a tendency to be easily bored or distracted.

*When your unicorn adds its light to number
five, you may experience runaway success
and good fortune. Your plans and projects
may be exciting and prosperous, for your
heart and soul are engaged in them.*

The Vibration of Number Six

Six is the vibration of the home-lover, the mother and father energy. It brings all the qualities of the responsible, committed and loving parent to any situation. So, it carries a caring, sympathetic, protective and nurturing energy. It sees things with compassion and empathy.

Number six influences you to be family and community-orientated. It enables you to be an excellent teacher, healer or carer. You bring artistic and creative energy to whatever you do.

The downside of this number is that you may be too self-sacrificing and self-effacing, so that you are put upon or may be inclined to rescue others.

> *When your unicorn adds its light to number six, you become the heart centre of your family or community and find soul satisfaction in creative expression. At the same time, you maintain a good sense of self-worth.*

The Vibration of Number Seven

Seven is the number of spirituality. It encourages you to seek truth through contemplation and meditation. It is the number of the intellectual, the bringer in of wisdom and new ideas.

The influence of this number may also cause you to withdraw into yourself, so that you can think, focus, analyse and try to understand life.

The downside of this number is that you may become too much of a hermit or too self-absorbed.

> *When your unicorn adds its light to number seven, it illuminates your inner world so that your quiet reflections bring you deep contentment and soul peace.*

The Vibration of Number Eight

Eight represents equilibrium. Its influence brings about balance between the material and the spiritual. This is a strong number that touches you with powerful ambition, big dreams and huge plans. If you are a leader or manager, it will give you the confidence, grit and determination to complete your project or vision, for you are goal-orientated. To assist this, you understand how the energy of money works. Because you are broadminded and you understand people, you forgive transgressions easily. This means those who work with you are on your side.

The downside of this number is that you may gamble away your money or opportunities.

*When your unicorn adds its light to
number eight, it enables you to become a
visionary or a successful business leader.*

The Vibration of Number Nine

Nine is the number of the idealist, the humanitarian and the philanthropist. If you are a high-minded politician, lawyer, writer, philosopher or genius, this number influences you to make huge efforts and give your all without looking for reward. You see beyond the parochial and can care for and give to the world.

This number also positively impacts architects, landscapers, creators and designers with creative and artistic energy. It helps bring people and situations together to be healed.

The downside of this number is that you may be aloof and feel superior.

> *When your unicorn adds its light to*
> *number nine, it encourages you to work*
> *or create for the good of humanity.*

Bathing in Number Pools with Unicorns

You can ask your unicorn to light up the cosmic pool of each number's vibration and then take you to bathe in it. This can light you up with the highest qualities of that number and make a significant impression on your life.

During this visualization your unicorn will take you to bathe in the vibration of your life path number. You can choose to experience a different number if you prefer.

ENTERING YOUR LIFE PATH NUMBER WITH YOUR UNICORN

~ Find a place where you can be quiet and undisturbed.

~ Close your eyes and ground yourself by sending roots from your feet into the heart of Lady Gaia.

~ You are sitting by a peaceful ocean under the light of a Full Moon and the sky is a twinkling blanket of stars.

~ Breathe yourself into a deeply relaxed space.

~ Gentle waves are lapping by your feet and you can see forever over the water.

~ Become aware of a shining white light like a sparkling diamond in the distance, getting bigger as it comes closer.

~ At last your unicorn stands in front of you, the waves softly splashing about its hooves.

~ Reach out to connect with it and thank it for coming to you.

~ Tell it that you wish to enter the vibration of your great cosmic life path number. Name the number.

~ Your unicorn immediately surrounds you in glorious pure white light.

~ You sit on its back and it wafts you dreamily through the cosmos.

~ Ahead you see an unimaginably huge ball of light, pulsating and shimmering, sending fingers of energy out to you. What colour is it?

~ In your cocoon of white light, your unicorn floats with you into the centre of the vibrating pool of your life path number.

~ You know it is influencing you for the highest good. It is subtly working on your energy centres so that the greatest possibilities for your journey on Earth are activated.

~ Relax and surrender. You are beyond time in this high-frequency space.

~ At last your unicorn withdraws with you from this cosmic light and streams back with you along a silver-white slide to where you started from.

~ Thank your unicorn and give yourself a little time to absorb fully what you have received.

Numbers don't only affect your life path. Through the workings of the great universal computer, you are drawn to a house, for example, because you have attracted its number energetically. People choose important dates, such as a wedding day, the day for the inauguration of a building, the start of a business or the holding of a special seminar, because of the cosmic influence of the number of that date. They may have figured this out consciously, but it will be equally pertinent and effective if it is seemingly random. Nothing is by chance.

Some numbers have a more powerful impact on your life path than others. These are known as master numbers.

Master Numbers

The master numbers are 11, 22, 33 and 44. (The other master numbers, 55, 66, 77, 88 and 99, do not affect the life path of anyone born in the current period.)

Examples:

- Date of birth: 1 November 2015. $1 + 1 + 1 + 2 + 0 + 1 + 5 = 11$

- Date of birth: 28 December 2016. $2 + 8 + 1 + 2 + 2 + 0 + 1 + 6 = 22$

- Date of birth: 7 September 1952. $7 + 9 + 1 + 9 + 5 + 2 = 33$

- Date of birth: 9 September 1979. $9 + 9 + 1 + 9 + 7 + 9 = 44$

How the master numbers influence your life path:

- *Eleven* is the number of the psychic or intuitive. It influences the sensitive and illuminates the clear channel. When your unicorn adds light to number 11, it gives you charisma as you search for spiritual insights and truths to help yourself and the world.

- *Twenty-two* is the powerful master-builder number. When your unicorn adds light to number 22, it helps you manifest your dreams, especially those that will benefit humanity.

- *Thirty-three* is the vibration of Christ consciousness. When your unicorn adds light to number 33, it brings about Oneness.

- *Forty-four* is the vibration of the Golden Era of Atlantis. When your unicorn adds light to number 44, it brings back the purity of that time and greatly accelerates your ascension and that of the planet. You start to remember your gifts and talents.

The master numbers hold a very high frequency and it is sometimes difficult to deal with their influence. If so, you can reduce 11 to 1 + 1 = 2, 22 to 2 + 2 = 4, 33 to 3 + 3 = 6 and 44 to 4 + 4 = 8.

Unicorn Guidance through Master Numbers

Unicorns often draw your attention to their presence through numbers, especially master ones. They also guide you through numbers, as follows:

- 11. Be a master and take responsibility for what you have created.

- 11:11. Start again at a higher level.

- 22. Start working towards your vision and build it on a solid foundation.

- 22:22. It is time to take action now.

- 33. Make sure you are acting with unconditional love.

- 33:33. Immerse yourself in Christ Light.

- 44. Live in the fifth dimension in harmony with all life forms, as you did in the Golden Era of Atlantis.

- 44:44. Bring back your gifts from Golden Atlantis.

- 55. Archangel Metatron is helping you on your ascension path.

- 55:55. Rise above your challenges and tune in to Archangel Metatron for assistance.

- 66. Remember you are much vaster than your little personality on Earth.

- 66:66. You are a being of the universe.

- 77. Live as your Higher Self, attuned at all times to the realms of angels, unicorns and ascended masters.

- 77:77. See with enlightened eyes.

- 88. Connect with your I AM Presence or Monad, your original divine spark from God.

- 88:88. Live to your highest potential.

- 99. Live as an ascended master.

- 99:99. You have learned the lessons of Earth.

Before you do this visualization, decide which of the master numbers you wish to enter, so that the vibration of that number can impact on and uplift your life.

ENTER THE VIBRATION OF A MASTER NUMBER WITH YOUR UNICORN

~ Find a place where you can be quiet and undisturbed.

~ See yourself sitting on a gently sloping hillside, overlooking a beautiful valley. Notice the view.

~ You are safe and comfortable and relaxed as you mentally call your unicorn.

~ It arrives in magnificent shimmering light and pours a stream of diamond light from its horn over you.

~ You tell your unicorn which master number vibration you wish to bathe in.

~ You mount your unicorn, who takes you up in a very fast ascension lift to higher dimensions of the cosmos.

~ You step from the lift and the high-frequency cosmic pool of your master number lies in front of you.

~ As you enter the pool, your unicorn illuminates you with multi-faceted light to help you absorb the vibrations.

~ You float dreamily in the pool, thinking of the highest qualities, energies or opportunities now available to you.

~ In divine right timing you leave the pool and return with your beloved unicorn to where you started from.

~ Notice if the view has changed in any way. Has it expanded? Is it more colourful? Are there more trees or animals? If so, it indicates that a change has already started to take place.

~ Thank your unicorn and open your eyes.

After this visualization, decide what you can do to enhance the influence of that master number in your daily life.

You may like to do this visualization before you go to sleep, so that the energy of the number can work with you overnight. You may choose to create a programme for yourself so that you work with all the numbers or master numbers at different times.

CHAPTER 11

Connecting to Unicorns through Models, Statues and Toys

When you have a model unicorn that you love and treasure, it isn't just an inanimate object, it's a focus through which your unicorn connects with you.

Eleanor told me this extraordinary story:

She has a little studio in her garden where she gives healing, reads oracle cards and does spiritual work with angels, unicorns and ascended masters. In it, she has a round glass table with a beautiful white unicorn on it and several packs of angel and oracle cards. One day she decided to have a reading from a medium called Stephen. She had never contacted him before and he knew nothing about her, but he tuned in to her as soon as she sat down and said, 'I am seeing a room full of ascended masters, angels and other beings of light. Do you have a sacred space in your home? There are lots of packs of oracle cards on a glass table.' Then he paused and was silent for a moment before he continued, 'I have been channelling for a very long time and what is occurring now has never happened before. A white unicorn has entered the room and is presenting himself. A pure white unicorn! Does that resonate with you?' Eleanor replied that it did. Stephen continued, 'He is bowing down and wants you to know that he is accepting the name you have given him.'

Eleanor had called the model unicorn on her glass table Pythagoras, Pi for short, and only that morning she had been asking him if he was happy with his name! Now she realized it was the name of her real personal unicorn as well and was absolutely delighted that he liked the name she had given him. The reading was a massive validation for her and helped her to know that her unicorn was with her.

Models, statues and toys of angels, fairies, dragons, animals and birds are all focus points through which the spirits of those beings connect with us. I remember visiting an elderly lady who was very fond of owls and she had a magnificent model owl that she absolutely adored on her coffee table. She would converse with him and had a real connection with him. One day she asked if I would like to talk to him. Rather embarrassed, I said, 'Of course I would,' and I telepathically asked the bird if there was anything he wanted to tell me. Rather to my surprise, the owl told me that the elderly lady had a daughter. Knowing she had never married, which was rather important in her generation, I was mind-blown and didn't quite know what to do. Tentatively, I asked her if she had ever had a baby. She denied it brusquely, so I assumed I had been wrong. Years later, I met her daughter. I really don't know why her owl gave me that information, but it certainly taught me the power of sacred statues.

We know that spirits can inhabit crystals, too, and the following story, from Gerda Widmaier, indicates that they can also inhabit certain toys.

One day Gerda was walking home past a clothes shop and decided to go in, but once inside, she didn't know why she was there. She wrote:

> *I saw a piece of clothing and went to the changing room with it, but it didn't fit and I didn't really like it. I pushed the curtain aside and saw several shelves of toys in front of me. I was just about to go, when suddenly I glimpsed hidden in the corner the wonderful plush head of a unicorn. I saw it and laughed, then bent down and pulled it out of the corner. It was a wonderful cuddly white unicorn. I pressed it to my heart and asked it whether it wanted to come home with me. It answered with 'Yes.' All the way home I felt happy and contented. It still gives me an indescribable feeling of contentment. It has become my protector and good friend.*

> *One night I was sleeping with my unicorn in my arms and dreamed that two wonderfully pure white unicorns came towards me. They were so beautiful and I had such a feeling of truth, I asked if they would tell me their names. They said, 'Fabio and Flora.' I felt overjoyed. A couple of days later, a Pegasus came to me in a dream and said its name was Clara. Since then I have really bonded with them all. They have a tremendously powerful energy and I feel every night when I go to sleep that I am surrounded by them. They envelop me in safety and security.'*

> *Marijke, who came on one of my retreats, told me about her connection with unicorns. Her 12-year-old son had been on a vacation with a group and as Marijke had listened to them all singing a unicorn song, she had felt that she had received unicorn*

energy. A few days later she had to go to Cologne to sell some jewellery. Next door to the jeweller's shop was a florist's and on the pavement in front of it was a huge white unicorn. Marijke was so enchanted by it that she went into the shop. There she found they had some small model unicorns and she felt impelled to buy one.

Afterwards she decided to do a meditation to connect with her personal unicorn. During the meditation she asked for its name and was given 'Jedai'. She felt really irritated by this, because she had never heard of this name and did not know how to spell it. So she meditated again several times to ask for her unicorn's name. Finally she was given the name 'Gerard'. This confused her at first, until she realized that there were two unicorns with her. Each had a different energy, for Jedai was feminine, while Gerard was masculine.

Weeks later she decided to ask if there really were two unicorns with her or if they were different aspects of the same unicorn. This time, to add to her confusion, she was given the name 'Duncan'! A third name! Furthermore, Duncan was a brown colour. When she meditated, she started to call, 'Jedai-Gerard-Duncan!'

That morning, before she told me this story, I had facilitated an exercise in pairs. While they had been working together, Marijke's partner, who had not known this story, had said to her that she had three unicorns with her. One was masculine, one feminine, and there was a little one too. She felt that they were her family and it was really important for her to know this.

Many people reported powerful experiences during that exercise. Here is what happened to Priti and her partner, Cina. Priti saw her unicorn as pure white sparkling light. It was a unicorn she was very familiar with and she said its name was Maya. She saw four unicorns round Cina and another above her. Cina also saw and felt four unicorns around her and one above her. They both felt a great surge of heat in their heart centre. I love it when people see or feel the same thing, as it offers such validation. Indeed, Priti told me afterwards that was exactly how she felt – validated.

Here is the exercise. You will need a partner to work with.

RECEIVING A UNICORN BLESSING

In this exercise, you and your partner take it in turns to offer each other a unicorn blessing.

~ Share what soul blessing each of you would like to receive. A soul blessing is something that will bring you soul contentment or satisfaction.

~ Stand in front of your partner and focus on their Earth Star chakra below their feet. Sense how big it is, what colour it is and if its chambers are open.

~ Call in Archangel Sandalphon to touch and ignite your partner's Earth Star chakra.

~ Bend down and physically bring the energy of their Earth Star up in a bubble around them, a Sandalphon Bubble. This opens their fifth-dimensional chakras and holds them open for a little while.

~ Invoke unicorns. Feel one touching your heart centre and hold up your hands until they feel filled with unicorn energy.

~ Then touch your partner's heart centre with your hands and let the unicorn energy flow into their heart.

~ As this happens, ask that they receive the blessing they want.

~   Receive any impressions.

~   When you have finished, stand back from your partner and cut away any energy you may have exchanged by making a cutting movement with your hands between you and your partner.

~   Share what you both experienced.

CHAPTER 12

Unicorns in Dreams

My friend Rosemary Stephenson told me that she had a model of a unicorn head that she kept in her bedroom. She explained that it had an incredible energy and when people came to workshops in her home, she placed it in the room where they were working. She said they always felt the energy and commented on it.

One night, six months after she had been given it, the head started to move. Not unnaturally, this caught her attention. Then it said to her telepathically three times, 'My name is Micah.' It continued, 'I have been with you for some time, but you haven't been tuning in to me.'

Rosemary immediately tuned in to him and realized he was helping to keep her vibration high.

Then she had a huge realization. A few years earlier, she had lived for a time on a farm with her niece, who had a tan-coloured horse called Spirit. He was a magnificent horse, like an Arab stallion, but very nervous, as he had been badly treated when young. In fact he was so stressed by people that he would never go to anybody. But when Rosemary met him for the first time they looked each other in the eye and knew each other at soul level. He immediately went to her and put his head on her head. She told me that he still did this whenever they saw each other. After she left the farm, she dreamed that Spirit came to her. But even though he was still tan, he had a white horn and was surrounded by a white aura. He said to her, 'My name is Micah.'

She responded, 'But you are Spirit!'

He replied, 'Spirit is my earthly name, but in the spirit world I am Micah.' And he turned white.

We live in a wondrous and magical universe.

Unicorns do give information in dreams. Jennifer Simis-Rapos wrote to me to say that her unicorn had showed her in a dream that I would be making a unicorn documentary and writing another book about them. It had showed her my thoughts about this and that I was very excited (which was true!) and said the unicorns were excited about it too. She had also been shown a nice man who would be helping me with the filming.

A year after she'd had the dream I mentioned during a Zoom workshop that I was making a unicorn documentary and writing this book. That was when she contacted me. When I received her e-mail, I had spoken to Dylan, the documentary-maker, but had not met him. A week later he came to my house and as he got out of the car I had an 'Aha!' moment and knew that this would be a good working connection. He was indeed a nice man.

Jennifer continued, 'After you mentioned this on the Zoom workshop, I had a dream that you were making a beautiful birthday cake. It had unicorns on top and you asked me if I would like a slice. I said, "*Yes!*" I also saw another birthday cake, but it wasn't yet ready.'

How fabulous! There is more to come.

Magic and healing can happen when a unicorn enters our dreams. Sarah e-mailed that she had always had an affinity with unicorns and from time to time they would come into her dreams quite prominently but gracefully.

She explained:

I suffered from very heavy periods for many years and because of a blood-clotting disorder was unable to take drugs and medication to help ease it. Other than having a hysterectomy, the only option was to have the Mirena coil inserted into my womb to help reduce the menstrual flow. I was reluctant to have this done, as I did not want a foreign device in my body. However, I was at my wits' end and, in the knowledge that many women got on fine with the coil in their body, agreed to have it inserted. Unfortunately, afterwards I experienced a lot of pain and also contracted an infection that made me quite ill, even though I was on a strong dose of antibiotics.

One night I went to bed in pain and with a fever. After a while I remember half waking from sleep, still slightly dazed but aware enough to feel my skin tingling and have the sensation that I was flying. I felt I was being carried safely under a unicorn's protective wings at high speed. The feathers of the wing that I was under were the purest white and tinged with blue. The flying unicorn told me telepathically, 'We are going to Lemuria.' I felt completely looked after, even though the wind was in my face as we travelled. It was as if we were beyond time and space and I felt safe enough to fall back asleep.

Upon waking the next morning, I remembered exactly what happened. I had never consciously heard of Lemuria before. I had heard of Atlantis, but not Lemuria. I researched it and it came to my awareness that much healing had occurred in Lemuria and that unicorns had been very much connected to it.

Over the next few weeks, my health started to improve and I had a great sense of being guided and looked after. I didn't have the coil removed straight away, but I know I received enough healing to improve my general health. I am very, very grateful to the winged unicorn.

It is so interesting that Sarah was given spiritual knowledge as well as an incredible experience while she was asleep. Indeed, Lemuria was the Golden Era before Atlantis. The beings there were etheric, not physical, and they acted as one, a great healing force that moved round the universe, touching places that needed wisdom and light. They had a particular love of Earth and nature. More than 260,000 years ago they knew that humanity would need their help during the 20-year period between 2012 and 2032 to prepare for the new Golden Age, so they created the amazing Lemurian healing crystals to light up individuals and the planet.

A dream about a unicorn can literally wake you up to your path. When Priti shared the following dream with me, she told me that for a long time she was too scared to look at the being who had come to her. This often happens, as people unconsciously sense a high vibration. Then, when they really see, everything transforms.

This is the story Priti told me:

I used to have a recurring dream in which I used to be carried in the night like a bundle. I felt too scared to look at who was carrying me and I didn't know why I was so scared. One night the familiar dream started and I told myself I was going to see who it was. I did so and to my amazement it was a unicorn, a shimmering white unicorn. Until that moment I hadn't known unicorns were real. I'd thought that they were imaginary beings.

From the moment I looked and saw the unicorn, I was wide awake. I knew it had come into my dreams to wake me up. Then I was able to get onto it and ride it. I didn't know where it was taking me until we arrived at a new house that was beautifully adorned with Christmas decorations. I didn't know this house, as it was somewhere totally new. I didn't know where it was. But it was a magical place and I knew the unicorn was taking me there to show me my future life.

Interestingly, Priti had a seemingly intractable problem to resolve in her life. She shared it with me and I reminded her that if she raised her frequency, everything could change, and I asked unicorns to help her for the highest good. A few days later she sent me an e-mail to say that magic had happened and a solution had been found.

> *Unicorns raise your frequency higher than that of a problem, so that it resolves.*

Sarah shared how a unicorn dream helped her heal a rift. Sarah and a friend fell out over a work issue. Sarah tried to sort it out, but her friend didn't wish to speak to her. The atmosphere was very strained and the lack of communication impacted on the smooth running of their work and affected the team around them.

A few days later Sarah went to bed feeling disheartened about the ongoing situation. That night she had a very vivid dream about a unicorn. Actually, it was a half-man half-unicorn: the upper body was that of a man with a long mane and the lower body was that of a unicorn. He was orange in colour and her friend was riding on him. He came to a halt outside her workplace and allowed her to get off and walk into work. She was carrying a basket. Then he turned and looked at Sarah, as she was also heading to their workplace, and she knew he was silently communicating to her that he was helping.

The next day when Sarah went into work, her friend still wasn't willing to talk things through. However, she did say hello and engage in pleasantries. She was also carrying a basket containing some cakes to share, including a cake for Sarah. Instantly, it reminded her of the dream in which the half-man half-unicorn had carried her friend and her basket into work!

After that, things started to improve between Sarah and her friend, even though they didn't speak about the contentious issue. Over time, they both started to let it go and 14 years later Sarah greatly values the fact that they are very good friends.

Sarah added that she had never seen a half-man half-unicorn in her dreams before, let alone one that was orange. Orange is a colour of warmth and friendship. Sarah said that although it was unusual to see the half-man half-unicorn, it was an utterly magical experience and she felt he very much stood for love, peace and resolution.

What an amazingly clear and practical dream message that unicorns were helping resolve the situation.

CALLING UNICORNS INTO YOUR DREAMS

If you would like to have unicorns in your own dreams, it is really helpful to think about them during the day so that you are receptive to their energy. Then, when you go to bed:

~ Have a glass of water by your bed.

~ Hold your hands over it and say or think, 'I bless you and call unicorns into my dreams.' Then drink it in anticipation.

~ Place a pad and pen by your bed.

~ Relax and affirm that you will remember your unicorn dreams.

~ Close your eyes and breathe comfortably.

~ Visualize a pure white unicorn in front of you.

~ Then let yourself drift into sleep.

~ When you wake, try to remember any dreams you have had and write down what you can.

~ Particularly write down any messages you have received.

~ Each time you do this you will almost certainly remember more and more, and this will bring you closer to your unicorn.

CHAPTER 13

Unicorns in Meditations

When you meditate, your right brain opens to other dimensions. It is much easier for you to access higher spiritual realms when you are in such a state. This is why visualizations are so powerful.

Erica Longden shared the following story with me:

I had always adored horses and as a child had spent every second I could around them. My family didn't have much money, so I offered to work in the yard of the local riding school to earn some riding lessons. It was no surprise that a unicorn deck was my first oracle deck. Oracle decks are quite magical and once I started opening up to unicorns, an amazingly powerful one came through to me in meditation. When I asked his name, instantly, as clear as a bell, I heard, 'Bucephalus'. I recognized the name as that of Alexander the Great's famous horse. He was so revered that he was buried in Jalalpur Sharif, outside Jhelum, in the Punjab, Pakistan.

That horse has now ascended as a unicorn and is always there if I call on him. I have such a strong connection to him, my heart bursts open just thinking of him. He was 'the king of horses, heart of a lion, swift as an eagle'. I am so honoured to have a connection to him. Sometimes it moves me to tears.

Like Bucephalus, unicorns can appear in an awesome way in meditations. Nathan, who had recently read *The Wonder of Unicorns*, e-mailed:

As I was performing my spiritual Yoga practice, from the serene mists of my meditation came an impressive (forgive me, words fail to capture the essence), mightily powerful unicorn. Suffice to say, I was awestruck. Striding right up to me with his beaming white body, lightning-coloured horn and so much grace, he rested his head next to mine so that our necks touched. We sat in this embrace as he enfolded me with his being – an ecstasy not of this world. It would take me months to unravel all that was given to me in that moment, and perhaps a lifetime. For, I later realized, this was my teacher making his presence known and telling me that guidance, lessons and tough tasks were on the horizon, but nonetheless I was firmly on the path for this life's mission.

Since that experience, he continued, he had been blessed to observe unicorns in meditation. Sometimes there were several of them frolicking playfully around rainbows and in other magnificent scenes.

He added that he was an infantry officer, rifle platoon leader and civil affairs officer as well as a deputy sheriff and pranic healer, and not used to sharing such experiences.

I am so grateful that he did share them.

Cina also told me that sometimes she felt the presence of unicorns. One day, when she had been meditating, she felt a huge opening appearing in front of her and a white light beaming onto her from a distance. It came closer and closer. Suddenly a huge unicorn stood in front of her. She said:

> *I was overawed when it telepathically asked me to ride it. We rose higher and higher into the air until we arrived at a palace in the 12th dimension. Round it there were 12 gemstones set to beam out light in each direction. A white lion appeared and escorted me on my unicorn into the centre of the palace. There I felt the presence and light of the unicorn very strongly. It was a very powerful experience and I woke up feeling I had been transformed.*

The lion represents masculine energy and the unicorn feminine. In addition, like the unicorn, the white lion carries Christ Light. It symbolizes Christ consciousness – pure unconditional love with strength.

The following story of an incredible meditation was sent to me by Bryan Tilghman. He shares it in one of his books, *Telos Welcoming New Earth.* He tells us that Telos is a city of crystal and light deep in the heart of Mount Shasta, California, and that Lemurians have always lived there, in the higher realms of the fifth dimension. I was so interested to read this, as the first time I visited Mount Shasta, the etheric retreat of Archangel Gabriel, I met several people who told me that their parents and grandparents used to talk of the tall, thin, gentle Lemurians who lived in the mountain and were occasionally seen out in the countryside.

In meditation Bryan travelled to the Pyramid in Telos, where Archangel Michael and two angels were waiting. He wrote:

Archangel Michael told me to come with him and that he had something to show me. I traveled with him in his energy field. His presence was strong but it was difficult to interpret the speed and distance of travel. I perceive that Archangel Michael simply directs his attention to a location and we are there. In an instant we stopped, and it felt as if we had traveled to the edge of the galaxy. There, we were looking out at the Milky Way from the perspective of Space. It was beyond beautiful, beyond description.

He asked if I was ready to go again and with a flash of light and in an instant I found myself in a field of tall grass staring up at a very large, white unicorn. He was standing very close to me with several others behind him. My mouth was hanging open and I did not know what to say. They communicated telepathically and I perceived them as very wise and kind beings. The first thing the unicorn said to me was, 'What, you didn't think we were real?' There were quite a few of them, perhaps six or seven, but one who was very close. He lowered his head so I could touch his face, and he appeared to me to be very similar to many of the images we see in our mythology. They are quite large and I perceived them to be nine or ten feet tall to the tops of their heads, with strong and muscular bodies. We were in the Fields of Telos. I could sense their great love and wisdom and it felt wonderful to be in their presence. He said they were coming back again to help us. He bid me a good day and said we would meet again.

Our inner journeys really do connect us with the magic of the cosmos.

Here is a very special and interesting story from Alicia Saa about a life-changing experience she had with a Pegasus and her unicorn during one of my online Zoom sessions. She wrote:

When we did the first meditation to connect with our unicorn, I was with my beloved unicorn, Whisper, and then a magnificent Pegasus came to me. My unicorn began walking towards him and sparks and lights shimmered in front of me. They became one and I knew a new frequency was available to me. When I asked for the Pegasus's name, he telepathically told me he came in representation of a Collective Unicorn energy and that I could call them 'P'. They would assist me in my mission to spread the teachings of advanced processes of forgiveness that carry the Christ Light. He added that I had been preparing my whole life for this and I was ready to lead by example with my teachings.

During the meditation in that Zoom session Archangel Gabriel brought his White Flame down over us. Then Serapis Bey followed with the White Flame of Atlantis. After this, we bathed in the Pools of Christ Light in Lakumay, the ascended aspect of Sirius.

Alicia added:

When I was immersed in Archangel Gabriel's White Flame and Serapis Bey's White Flame of Atlantis, I had a deep feeling of purification and cleansing. I felt that this was needed to receive the Christ Light in the fifth, seventh and ninth-dimensional pools. Every pool had a different vibration, colour and sound. The one that made a profound impact on me was the ninth-dimensional pool. When I was bathing in that pure and pristine energy, I heard myself declaring, 'God, I only want you,' and all my worldly desires vanished within the pool. At that moment I knew I was ready for something extremely beautiful.

After that, when I arrived at the Unicorn Kingdom I found myself in the presence of the King and Queen of the Unicorns and they blessed me and infused me with all the qualities that I need to carry to fulfil my soul mission. Finally I came back to Earth with the Collective Unicorn Energy that was assigned to me and two baby unicorns who will teach me how to nourish, balance and take care of my body in the most loving way so I can proceed to fulfil my soul mission. It was a wonderful session and I just wanted to share with you part of my journey.

CONNECTING WITH UNICORNS IN MEDITATION

~ Look back over these stories of people's experiences with unicorns during meditation and choose one that particularly touches you.

~ Close your eyes and take yourself through that journey.

~ You may follow the same path but you may find yourself having an entirely different experience.

~ Write your experience down in your unicorn journal.

CHAPTER 14

Unicorns in Nature

Although unicorns usually appear in dreams and meditations or in that period between waking and sleeping when the veils between the dimensions are very thin, people also see them out in nature in beautiful spots where the frequency is high and the energy pure, for in these places, too, the veils between the worlds are thin.

I would like to offer some of the stories that people have shared of seeing a unicorn with their physical eyes.

Leonie van Veghel sent me a wonderful e-mail about her first experience with a unicorn. It had taken place the previous day when she had been out in the woods near her house. She told me there was a special place there where you could cross a little bridge and enter a fairy wood. Two big trees were there, one either side of the portal, and it felt as if they were guardians at a doorway. This was a very sacred, magical place, so over time Leonie had sent gratitude and love to it and also brought offerings.

She explained that the previous morning she had met a friend who was very sick and stuck in unhelpful old patterns. After the meeting she felt heartbroken because she wanted to help, but her friend wasn't open to the love and light she was sending to her. The only place she could go was her place in the woods. She communicated with the elementals there, then she went to the fairy wood. She wrote:

> *It was then and there that a unicorn appeared. It was radiating indescribable white light, the brightest light imaginable. I was standing on a little path and the unicorn was standing between trees some distance away. It was giving me white energy and also white energy with rainbows. The rainbows were somehow important. It was also giving me hope. This was a clear message. I'll remember for the rest of my life the brightness of the light that the unicorn radiated. It truly was beyond words. Then, when I rode my bike out of the woods, very special energy came from above and flushed me clean. It really felt as though it had cleansed me. I thought,* Just let go, let it wash away all that needs to be washed away. Allow it to cleanse you.

Leonie felt that this was a gift from the unicorn.

However, the unicorn connection didn't end there. Later that day the unicorn appeared in Leonie's living room. It came very close to her, putting its head on her heart area as she sat curled up on the couch.

She added, 'Then the unicorn was standing in the living room giving me white light. I was so open and in such a very vulnerable place that I could receive it. We shared a very special day yesterday at our first meeting.'

Unicorn encounters are life-changing.

Here is the story of a unicorn encounter that was sent to me by Essa Love, who e-mailed:

I'm an energy healer from Germany. I'm very happy and so excited to write to you about my unicorn experiences. On 19 January 2018, I saw a unicorn for the first time. Before that I had not paid any attention to them. It was like this. I chatted with a friend one day and wanted to see if they really existed. That night I lit a candle in the living room. Before I meditated, I prayed that I might see a unicorn if they really existed. I didn't see anything in meditation. But the moment I opened my eyes I saw a beautiful, tall and majestic white horse flashing with silvery white light very close to me. His two front legs had silver-like bracelets on them. He didn't seem to be an ordinary unicorn. His energy field was very sacred and solemn, like that of a king. Beneath his power I felt he was very compassionate.

This encounter opened Essa up to the unicorn realms and she saw others after this one, but she says that the beauty of this first unicorn was different from that of the others.

Most people who love horses are automatically connected to unicorns. Katie certainly is. She explained that she grew up riding ponies and she and her sisters looked after their own. As a child, she also played with her fairy friends and elementals in the garden. She told me that the county of Dorset, in the south of the UK, had a strong unicorn energy! I was delighted to hear this, for it was there that I had my first unicorn encounters.

Katie also told me about her sister's horse, Walter, who was a large thoroughbred. Apparently he was very special and had a real presence. He also had a 'Prophet's thumbprint' on his neck. This is a birthmark like an indentation found on the neck or chest of a horse. According to legend, the Prophet Mohammed was in the desert once with his herd of Arabian horses. They became very thirsty and when they reached a watering hole, he set them free. They ran to drink, but before they could do so, he called them back. Only five of the mares stopped and returned to him without satisfying their thirst. It is said that to thank them for their loyalty and obedience, he blessed these five mares by pressing his thumb into their necks. They were kept for breeding, and horses like Walter, with thumbprints, are believed to be descendants of these mares and to be lucky.

Katie shared: 'Walter belonged to my eldest sister, Sarah, and she loved him very much. I started to ride him in my early teens. Once as I was riding him, Walter heard a hunting horn being blown and bolted with me. We ended up hitting an articulated lorry. We were both unharmed but very shaken. Soon after this we discovered he had fused vertebrae in his spine. This was operated on but sadly it was unsuccessful and he had to be put down.'

She explained to me how in those days a bolt and hammer were used to put a horse to sleep. The bolt entered the horse's head at the exact point where a unicorn's horn would be. This is the point where Katie believes a horse has a cosmic connection to unicorns.

Understandably, Sarah could not hold Walter while he was put down. The vet had always treated him and he, too, was very attached to him. So Katie decided she would be brave and hold him. As he was shot and his body fell to the ground, she saw what she now thinks was his unicorn essence – multicoloured energy that spiralled down and back up again. She believed it had come to get his soul.

She added, 'This was when I realized that perhaps many horses were connected to unicorns and when placing our hands on this sacred area below the forelock, we could reactivate the connection.'

Katie is a medical acupuncturist and she continued:

I established my clinic in 2005. I have moved three times since then and the last move happened very suddenly. I really wasn't happy about it, as I had spent so much money on my previous place. I sat at home and asked my angels, unicorns and guides to find me a place and fast. Within an hour I had a message from a lady I knew through horse-riding. She told me her husband was currently renting a beautiful Georgian house in town and was putting it on the market that day. I went immediately to look at it, and as soon as I entered, I was blown away by unicorn energy. Unicorns literally appeared in a counter-clockwise circle in the entrance hall, singing, 'Yes.' I knew absolutely this was the place for me. The landlord was so lovely and we struck a deal quickly.

She says that many people comment as soon as they enter the building on the wonderful welcome they feel. A dear friend walked in and remarked, 'You do know you have four or five unicorns in the hallway?'

When she heard that, Katie jumped up and down with delight. That friend isn't the only person to have felt the unicorns there and Katie believes they protect the place and also heal people as they enter and leave the building.

I regularly do an 'Angel Inspiration Hour' on Facebook Live. One week Aingeal shared that she had seen a unicorn in a field very early one morning:

I was in a taxi on the way to Gatwick airport. I had given a workshop the night before and unicorns had come in. The taxi driver was playing bhajans, which I love, and so I was in a meditative state. I was just looking out of the window and saw a small white horse in a field. I was thinking, What is that little horse doing by itself in the middle of nowhere? Its head was down, but when it lifted it, there was the horn. I was astonished and wanted to stop, but we were on the motorway and the driver did not speak much English, so I just watched it until it was out of sight. I will never forget it.

I was so thrilled when I read Aingeal's story. Bhajans are devotional spiritual songs and I too love them. Some of my most sacred memories are of joining in singing bhajans in India. And unicorns are everywhere. We see them when we are in the right space and where the veils are thin.

CHAPTER 15

Unicorn Orbs

A ngelic beings, including unicorns, are able to bring their vibration down to the sixth dimension so that it can be captured by a camera. Accordingly, certain scientists have been inspired by their angels and higher guides to create digital cameras that operate on the matching vibration. So, Orbs are the sixth-dimensional light bodies of angelic beings and their appearance in photographs was orchestrated by the spiritual kingdom to give us physical proof of the presence of the angelic realms.

Originally people dismissed Orbs as drops of moisture or specks of dust on the lens of the camera, but scientists now agree that there is an energy source in each one. This coincides with mystics' understanding that Orbs have a spiritual source.

Understanding Orbs

Usually Orbs appear in photographs quite unexpectedly. However, you can also call them in in the same way that you can invoke angels or unicorns.

Some people are particularly adept at tuning into a unicorn and calling it in to be seen as an Orb on their pictures. Whether or not you catch a unicorn in a photograph depends on your energy, though, so here are a few pointers:

- Unicorns and angels respond to an open heart. So you must be open-hearted to take a photograph with an Orb in it.

- Your frequency as a photographer must match that of the being you call in.

- Vitality and excitement raise your frequency.

- Being relaxed is important.

- A single Orb may appear, or a few, or hundreds.

- Their shape and colour are meaningful.

Different Kinds of Orb

We are always surrounded by spiritual beings who are on different wavelengths from us and therefore invisible to most of us. These include fairies, elementals, angels, spirits of the departed, ghosts, spirit guides, ascended masters and of course unicorns. One of the reasons that so many Orbs are appearing in photographs now is that the veils between the dimensions are becoming thinner.

I have seen thousands of angels, archangels and Angels of Love in photographs. Angels are usually opaque white unless they are actively protecting someone, in which case they are transparent. Archangels are different colours, while Angels of Love, who generously accompany archangels out of pure love, are brilliant white.

Understanding Unicorn Orbs

As I studied thousands of Orbs, I learned which ones were unicorns, and Kumeka taught me more about them. They are often found working in harmony with angels and appearing even lighter and brighter than they are. Sometimes they are vast and opaque, while at other times they are small and clear, and often near to someone. They also travel to rescue people who are in danger from negative energy. I remember an Orb of Archangel Michael merging with that of a unicorn and racing to help someone, leaving a trail of energy flowing behind it as it was moving so fast. It wasn't in a photograph taken seconds earlier. I learned that angels and unicorns take only one thousandth of a second to move into place!

I have seen awesome pictures of several unicorns drifting together across the sky and being captured as pure white Orbs. Some of those in the distance appeared as shining white pinpricks of light.

As unicorns come nearer to you, they have to step down their energy, as otherwise it would be too much for you, and then they appear as a soft or even faint white Orb. If you look at one, you will pick up their extraordinary light. Because a wave of Christ Light flows into our planet during Christmas, you will receive an extra download of unicorn light if you focus on a unicorn Orb at that time. It is also a special time for unicorns to visit individuals or families.

Invoking a Unicorn Orb

Here is a wonderful story that illustrates how you can invoke unicorn Orbs. Essa Love wrote:

An impressive and amazing moment happened in April 2018 when I was meditating in the garden. I told the unicorns that I wanted them to appear in my photos, set the camera to automatic capture mode and then closed my eyes and asked them to come. When I looked at the photos, I was surprised to see their light revolving round me!

Essa attached a picture of herself meditating in the garden surrounded by a huge unicorn Orb! It was incredible. She added: 'Since then unicorns have played a very important role in my life and have fulfilled many wishes for me. For example, I wanted to go on a trip to Egypt to study, but I didn't have enough money. I asked the unicorns to help me with my travel plans. Two weeks later my uncle visited me and during our chat I told him about my hopes. He asked me how much it would cost. When I told him, he immediately said he would assist me in financing it. I was really happy! Suddenly, a unicorn appeared in my mind and I realized that it had really aided me. The unicorns' pure high frequency always brings me happiness and protection. They also remind me to take care of my inner child and keep my childlike sense of wonder. At this moment, as I am writing to you, I can feel them around me and it brings tears to my eyes. I feel blessed and very grateful for their help and encouragement.'

Unicorn Energy Balls

As well as invoking unicorn Orbs, you can make a unicorn energy ball in your hands with focused attention. Here you are calling in unicorn light to form a pure white globe, for a round shape can hold more high-frequency energy than any other.

MAKING A UNICORN ENERGY BALL

~ Cup your hands together facing each other in front of you.

~ Invoke your unicorn and ask it to pour light from its horn into a ball between your hands.

~ As it does so, you may find your hands tingling or becoming warm.

~ Place the ball over any part of your body, ask it to raise your frequency and feel its energy entering you. You can also send it to a person or place that needs to be touched by unicorn light.

~ Thank your unicorn.

MAKING A UNICORN AND ARCHANGEL ENERGY BALL

It is a wonderful feeling to call in the energy of an archangel to merge with unicorn light. You can call in any of the archangels to merge with unicorn energy in a ball, following the procedure above.

~ When you invoke the emerald Archangel Raphael with a unicorn to create a white-green Orb, it has great healing power. It is also incredibly effective for opening up to clairvoyance or abundance. You can send it to someone in need if you wish.

~ Just think of the impact of creating a white-blue Orb filled with Archangel Michael and unicorn energy, then placing it in your throat chakra for higher communication or to purify your powers of telepathy. You can send it to someone who needs courage or to a place that needs protection.

~ Try making a white-pink Orb of love with an Archangel Chamuel and unicorn vibration.

CHAPTER 16

Unicorn Card Readings

Oracle card readings are very popular and have been for a long time. Even in the Golden Era of Atlantis, families would do Tarot readings together. It was considered a way of learning more about yourself and others so that you could take wise decisions for the benefit of all.

Unicorn cards are pure and high frequency, so they tune you in to your Higher Self or the soul of the person you are reading for, rather than the desire body.

While I am waiting for a Facebook Live or online Zoom class to begin, I often do card readings for people or a general reading.

Alicia is one of the regular followers of my programmes, so when she asked for a unicorn card reading, I shuffled the deck and asked the unicorns to bring forward the perfect message for her. She e-mailed later:

> *You chose a card for me ... and it was the King of the Unicorns. I was jumping up and down, because in the last Unicorn Zoom you took I found myself in the presence of the King and Queen of*

the Unicorns and they blessed me and infused me with all the
qualities that I need to fulfil my soul mission.

She added that she connected very easily with unicorn energy at
Full Moon and had taken some pictures of the Moon after the
Zoom, but hadn't looked at them. She continued:

Later I had the impulse to look for those pictures on my phone.
When I saw the first one, I decided to enlarge it and the energy
almost knocked me out. I felt the magnificent and majestic
presence of the King of the Unicorns. Wow! Wow! Wow! In the
picture the Moon had disappeared totally and his energy had
taken over. I showed it to Emmanuelle, my youngest son, and he
was ecstatic. He told me, 'Mom, when you recover your freedom
[I am undocumented in the USA at the moment], we are going to
London to find Diana so we can say thank you.

Oh, bless him. I am looking forward to meeting them one day.
When I read the e-mail, I couldn't wait to look at the amazing
photograph attachment. In *Enlightenment Through Orbs* there is
a photograph of the Full Moon surrounded by unicorn energy.
Kumeka has confirmed that unicorn energy is enormous, much
larger than the Moon, and indeed, when I looked at Alicia's
photograph, she was right: the blazing light of the King of the
Unicorns entirely engulfed the Moon.

Recently several people have talked to me about meeting
the King and Queen of the Unicorns during meditations,
visualizations or dreams. As their title would suggest, these
are the most awesome and highest-frequency unicorns that we
can connect with. The King blesses us with majesty, vision and
power, while the Queen offers love, compassion and wisdom.

They then expect us to act with the dignity and higher qualities that we have received.

All unicorns can bless our hopes and dreams through unicorn cards and help to bring them about. Elizabeth had a dream of owning a holiday property in a foreign country. She could picture it in her mind's eye. However, it felt like a fantasy and she wondered if it would ever happen Then some extra cash became available, so she decided to enjoy a holiday in the Italian Lakes and look at properties at the same time.

At that point she went to the London Mind, Body, Spirit festival. That year the Diana Cooper School had taken a stall and some of our highly gifted teachers had volunteered to give unicorn card readings. Elizabeth asked for a three-card reading. The teacher asked what she wanted to know about, so Elizabeth told her she was going on a holiday to Italy that she was combining with looking at holiday apartments. Her reading had the prosperity card, the wishing well and the freedom card! The reader told her there was nothing to stop her: she would buy a property. So she flew to Italy and viewed three properties. She wrote:

> The last property was an apartment in a building. However, it had lovely views of a lake and hills. The person who owned it showed me around. She had exactly the same cushions that I had. She also had a figurine of a character that I had several of at home. I had a discussion with another family member and we decided to go for it. I now own it and have had many happy holidays there. I have a unicorn picture on one of its walls. I know that unicorns made this dream a reality. I know they gave me a blessing with the reading I had, and the cards were right. The road where the property is situated is called 'the Road of

the Horses' and there is a picture on the wall of a knight riding a white horse.

Giving Unicorn Card Readings

Many of you will already be proficient and probably inspired spiritual card readers, but for those of you who doubt your ability, remember this: if you are reading this book, you can almost certainly tune in to unicorns to do unicorn card readings!

Preparation

Before you start, it is, however, important to get to know your unicorn cards and tune in to them. First hold the deck in your hand and feel it. Then look at the individual cards and get a sense of each one.

You also need a special cloth on which to lay out your reading and in which to wrap the deck.

A Three-Card Reading

There are many kinds of reading. The simplest is a three-card one. For this reading, you just take three cards. The first represents the past, the second the present and the third the future.

GIVING A THREE-CARD READING

~ Light a candle if possible, dedicated to the unicorn card reading.

~ Hold the deck and tune in to it.

~ Bless the cards. Something simple like 'Unicorns, please bless these cards for the highest good' is fine, though you can add whatever feels right.

~ Ask the person you are reading for if they have any questions.

~ Spread out the cards on the special cloth and ask the person you are reading for to pull out three cards with their non-dominant hand.

~ As you look at the first card, you might like to unfocus your eyes and receive an impression. What jumps out at you? What are you drawn to?

~ Just say what comes into your head. The less you censor the messages that come through, the clearer your channel.

CHAPTER 17

Service Work with Unicorns

In my seminars and online courses we often do service work, and this is very popular, because all lightworkers have incarnated to assist the planet. I find that people particularly love sending unicorns to help, heal and illuminate the world. Like all beings of light, unicorns are always delighted to do our behest for the highest good of all.

Service work makes your light brighter.

Here are some suggestions for service work with unicorns to make the world a better place.

BLESSING WATER

When you ask with a pure heart for unicorns to bless water, it adds divine qualities and Christ Light to it. If you then pour it into a stream, river, the sea or even down the drain, it will spread and raise the energy of the entire area. It is wonderful if you can do this physically, but if you can't, then visualize it happening.

~ As well as simply asking unicorns to add their light to water, you can ask them to add a specific quality to it, such as joy or tranquillity. Then know that this quality will affect people, animals, trees and anything that is touched by the water.

~ Thank the unicorns.

SENDING UNICORNS TO A PLACE THAT NEEDS PEACE

Sadly, there are still many parts of the world where egos are clashing so much that people cannot see the oneness.

~ Think of one such place.

~ Call in unicorns. Hundreds or thousands may come to you.

~ Imagine a bridge of light going from your heart to that town or country.

~ Ask the unicorns to take peace to this area.

~ See them flying like a cluster of diamonds across the bridge as directed.

~ First they pour light from their horns over the entire area, showering it in peace.

~ Then they fly down and touch the hearts of the children there with serenity.

~ See this tranquil feeling spreading from the children to their families.

~ Visualize a dome of peace over the area and ask that it be anchored there.

~ Thank the unicorns.

WELCOMING BABIES

In the Golden Era of Atlantis, every soul coming into incarnation was wanted, invited and welcomed. This is no longer the case and many babies are born with their hearts partially or even fully closed as a result.

~ Think of a particular baby, or a maternity ward, or those babies who have been born into less than ideal circumstances.

~ Invoke hundreds of unicorns and sense them gathering around you.

~ Open your heart and send out pink rays of light to the babies.

~ Ask the unicorns to link to the little ones through this pink light and touch their hearts with pure love.

~ Send out a prayer that these babies may start their lives with love, joy and happiness.

~ See the unicorns blanket every baby in a pure white-pink cocoon of love.

~ Thank the unicorns.

HELPING PEOPLE WHO FEEL MISUNDERSTOOD

Millions of people in the world feel that no one understands them. They feel that their motives are questioned, their good intentions doubted and that no one really knows who they are or how they feel. Entire communities feel isolated and misunderstood. It is important that we return to oneness so that we can know who people truly are. One of the ways we can help is to ask unicorns to touch the hearts of humanity, so that all religions, cultures and peoples accept and learn to understand one another.

~ Create a huge ball of angel energy.

~ Ask Archangel Uriel, angel of confidence and wisdom, to pour golden light into it.

~ Then ask Archangel Chamuel, angel of love, to add pink light.

~ See the gold and pink light merging so that the ball shimmers with the peach of love and wisdom.

~ Ask unicorns to stream their diamond-white light into it.

~ Then direct the unicorns out into the world with balls of the white-peach light.

~ See them placing these balls of love, peace and oneness into the consciousness of all those who feel misunderstood.

~ See them bringing the world together in love and understanding.

~ Thank the unicorns.

SENDING WISDOM AND LIGHT TO ALL SCHOOLS AND TEACHERS

It would help the world evolve if all teachers acted and taught with wisdom. There are children and students everywhere longing to be inspired by wise ones. Archangel Jophiel is the pale yellow archangel of wisdom, and when he works with unicorns, incredible things can happen.

~ Invoke unicorns and Archangel Jophiel.

~ Ask them to merge their light to pour it into the minds of teachers world-wide.

~ See a glorious yellow-and-white light flowing.

~ Bring to mind a school, college, university or individual student or teacher.

~ Watch the white-yellow light of the unicorns and Archangel Jophiel's angels fill the mind(s) of the student(s) or teacher(s) you have thought of.

~ Then see the light spreading through educational establishments in every country of the world.

~ See students alive with interest and wanting to learn.

~ Thank the unicorns and Archangel Jophiel.

CREATING AND WORKING WITH A PORTAL

A portal is a high-frequency space that can be dedicated to a particular purpose. It can be a doorway through which angelic beings step into your home, or people and animals pass over safely and beautifully, or a place of healing, love, joy or whatever you feel impressed to focus on. When you create a portal, the angels or unicorns of those who need that energy or quality will take them to bathe in it during their sleep. Then magic can happen.

To make a portal, you set your intention to create one. This is particularly effective when a group is working together with a common focus. You can build a portal anywhere in the world and do not need to be near it. Some portals, like those in sacred places, last eternally. Others may last for hours or days or longer. Set the duration you wish yours to be active. You may need to continue to energize it if it is long term.

CREATING A UNICORN PORTAL

~ Decide what kind of portal you wish to create.

~ Mentally say, 'I now create a unicorn portal for [state the purpose].'

~ Invoke unicorns.

~ Visualize light building up. It may be a column, a flame or any other shape.

~ See the unicorns pouring pure diamond-white light with your dedicated quality into it.

~ You have now formed a unicorn portal for a higher purpose and the unicorns are holding the energy.

~ Sense or see people, animals and other beings from the universe being brought by their angel or unicorn to bathe in this portal.

~ Ask the unicorns to protect it and look after it.

~ State how long you want your portal to remain in place and active.

~ Thank the unicorns.

ADDING UNICORN LIGHT TO THE PORTAL OVER TABLE MOUNTAIN

Abundance is a state of consciousness that attracts all you need for your highest happiness and good. Table Mountain in Cape Town, South Africa, is already a vast portal for abundance that is waiting to be opened so that the consciousness of plenty can spread over Africa and then the world. When you ask unicorns to add their light to it, it will help the world to become prosperous and happy more quickly.

~ Invoke unicorns and sense several coming to you.

~ Ask them to add their light of abundance to the portal over Table Mountain in Cape Town.

~ Visualize a glorious rainbow flowing from your heart centre to Table Mountain.

~ See unicorns pouring light over the mountain.

~ See a golden door above the mountain opening wider.

~ Let more and more golden light cascade through the door and spread to all the people in South Africa.

~ See all the people being happy, prosperous, at peace and connected to one another.

~ Then watch the light spread round the world.

~ Thank the unicorns.

You can send unicorns and their light anywhere on the planet or even in the cosmos in any way that you wish. Here are a few more suggestions:

- Send unicorn light into the minds of all those who are ready to live in a fifth-dimensional spiritual way.

- Send unicorn light to bring about world-wide integrity and honesty.

- Send a ball of unicorn light into the third eyes of all those who are ready to see from a higher perspective.

- Send a ball of unicorn light into the Earth Star chakras of humanity to light up the blueprint of their higher potential.

- Send unicorn energy to light up people's soul gifts so they can enjoy a life of fulfilment, soul satisfaction and contentment.

- Create a unicorn portal of light from the planet into the heavens through which stuck souls can pass easily.

- Pour unicorn light into the minds and hearts of all so that they treat animals with loving care.

CHAPTER 18

Magical Unicorn Stories

Tim Whild is an old friend of mine, a clairvoyant and medium who works on a very high frequency and has seen many unicorns. I asked him about this and he told me that his first unicorn experience was in spring 2015.

'It was the night of the spring equinox,' he said. 'I was looking up at the starlit sky when I saw a huge cross of light appearing, almost like a Christian cross. It was a Stargate opening.'

A Stargate is a portal of very high-frequency energy through which light connects to the Earth. It raises the vibration, so it changes people's lives everywhere.

Tim continued, 'I saw hundreds of thousands of unicorns in streams of light pouring through the Stargate. There may have been millions of them.'

I asked him what they looked like and he told me, 'I saw them as traditional pure white horses with horns of light moving through in stream after stream, but there were so many I could hardly tell them apart. They were almost linked together. It was something so incredible I will remember it for the rest of my life.'

'Why were they coming?'

'They were coming to help the planet and to enable individuals to move into a higher state of being.'

'Did they tell you this?'

'No, I just knew it. They didn't communicate. I was just witnessing.'

Tim then told me of an awesome occasion when unicorns did communicate with him. 'Two years later I was lying on the sofa in my lounge, looking out of the big sash window. It was a stormy night and I was watching the wind blowing in the trees. Suddenly my vision was filled with myriads of very bright points of light. They were not normal lights – they were so luminous, they were like tiny suns. They spoke to me. In a normal voice, just as I'm speaking now. They introduced themselves by saying, "We are unicorns. We are coming in at a very high frequency now." They told me that their vibration had gone up. On the previous occasion they had been in an angelic form that was very pure and high. However, now it was even higher and they were like flying diamonds.'

The unicorns added, 'We are using your crystal to anchor ourselves in.' They were referring to a beautiful Lemurian crystal that Tim still has.

I asked him if this visitation had affected his life and he replied, 'It was the first time I'd seen anything so incredible. And it changed my year. All of a sudden my pathway went from mediocre to very high frequency. Everything changed. My work changed. I didn't sleep for three nights because the unicorns kept on coming. It was like being plugged into the mains. In the end I asked them to slow down!'

I enquired if it had affected his relationships, but he shook his head. 'No, it was more that it transformed my relationship with the spiritual. That changed dramatically. It opened my eyes to much higher possibilities. Things people had talked about I had seen with utmost clarity.'

Here is another extraordinary unicorn story, which was told to me by Kirsty Wade:

About three years ago, I went on a spiritual retreat weekend. During one of the meditation sessions I suddenly met my unicorn in his full glory! I knew his name was Orion and he had communicated with me before, but this was different. In my mind's eye, it was as if a film had started playing and I could see everything so clearly.

Suddenly I was riding on the back of Orion and we were flying through the universe, through the amazing stars and galaxies, and it was truly wonderful! He took me to a place I can only describe as magical. It seemed as though all the souls, angels, spirit guides, animal spirits and beings of light who were important in my life were there. They were all gathered round me in a circle and they all appeared as pure white beings, whiter than I had ever known white could be. They stood in front of what was the most magical autumn backdrop I had ever seen: blazing, bright, colourful trees. Stunning... I seemed to be lying down, as the view I had was from that perspective. My guide stood over me and communicated two clear words to me, which were 'initiation' and 'operation'. Very quickly after this, the meditation session ended and so did my vision. I felt amazing! I knew something very important had just happened. However, I didn't pay enough attention to the two words I had been given!

At this time, my husband and I had started trying to have a baby. A few weeks after my retreat I was out doing some Christmas shopping when I suddenly started feeling intense pain in my abdomen. It was so intense I could barely stand up and I knew something was wrong, so I called myself an ambulance and was taken to hospital. I ended up having emergency surgery due to an ectopic pregnancy. When I woke up after the surgery, the surgeon told me they'd had to remove one of my Fallopian tubes. I was so upset.

I was wheeled back through to the ward that night feeling very sore and wondering what had just occurred. Then the nurses left the room and something amazing happened: all of a sudden, standing right beside my bed were my unicorn, Orion, and Archangel Gabriel! They both appeared in that wonderful, ethereal shade of white that just doesn't seem to exist on Earth! I knew it was Archangel Gabriel, as he introduced himself, and I had already met Orion! Archangel Gabriel told me very clearly that this 'had to happen' to me and that it had to happen before 30 December (I'm still not entirely sure why). At the same time, Orion was dipping his head and directing a beautiful beam or 'horn' of light right at my abdomen, where I'd had my surgery. I can't tell you how amazing this felt! The healing beam truly did stop the pain I was feeling and Archangel Gabriel's words somehow gave me instant relief too. I knew that there must be an important reason why this had happened to me and from that moment on, I accepted it.

Nurses would periodically visit my bed to check fluids, etc., and at those points, Orion and Archangel Gabriel would disappear, but then reappear as soon as they'd left. It was so comforting for me having them there. I remember pinching myself to make sure I wasn't dreaming, but I absolutely knew I wasn't! It was so magical, I didn't want to go to sleep. The pain relief from Orion was truly a gift. Both Orion and Archangel Gabriel stayed with me until I went fully to sleep that night.

When I woke up the next day I just wanted it to be night-time again so they would be by my side! As I lay in bed that day, it suddenly occurred to me that I'd had an operation and I remembered the words I'd been given during my vision at the retreat weekend: 'initiation' and 'operation'. That was the operation! And I knew that the experience must be part of an initiation for me. The message suddenly made sense! How amazing!

I had much healing to do after this, but the magical experience I'd had with Orion and Archangel Gabriel gave me immense comfort, hope and optimism for the days ahead. I'm overjoyed to say that almost exactly a year to the day later, I found out I was pregnant with our beautiful daughter, Annabella. We have just celebrated her first birthday!

Overlit by Unicorns

Kumeka teaches that when your original divine spark, or Monad, leaves Source, it is programmed to hold angelic energy, especially that of archangels and unicorns. As it sends out souls, each one of them contains some of that angelic light. When you incarnate, that energy is within you; it is your birthright, waiting to be tapped. As you raise your frequency and more of your soul energy becomes available to you, more of your angelic essence does too.

Kumeka also teaches that when your heart is wide open to them, beings of light can come right into you. In one week I had a long conversation with a lady who believed she was a unicorn and another who knew she was a fairy and I was absolutely amazed to receive this inspiring story from April Aronoff:

In early February I was downstairs in my indoor temple space. I was standing up when all of a sudden my world shifted and I had a horn on my head and hoofs at the end of my legs. The knowing that I was a unicorn completely overcame me, but it was over in a split second. I didn't give it any more thought and went back to whatever I had been doing.

Later in the month I had a couple of hours to myself and was going back and forth from my indoor temple space to the garden, pruning, weeding and talking to my plants. I remember it was a beautiful sunny day, warm for February. I was coming indoors from the garden when again my world began to shift. I felt myself in two places at the same time, with the floor, walls and ceiling beginning to tilt and become fuzzy. I remember pressing my hands against the walls to try to stabilize myself. It was as if my 3D world was falling away, so I picked myself up and stumbled outside. As I did this, an entire collection of memories came rushing in – of being a unicorn and my entire race being hunted and killed for their horns. A giant wave of grief came rushing in too, and I ended up on my hands and knees in the garden, sobbing uncontrollably as the memories overcame me.

Afterwards I stood up with a tremendous amount of energy pulsing through me. I felt intense divine love for these beautiful beings that I knew from that moment were part of me. The Christ love that is the unicorn itself had cracked me open from the inside out. My senses were heightened during this time and I could see, hear and taste with much more intensity than before.

I began to work with unicorns daily. In fact since that time I have never been without them. One unicorn in particular, Krystal, has presented himself as my personal ally and guide. He is always with me now. Sometimes he is powder blue and sometimes he is white. I absolutely love him! Other unicorns live in my garden, along with dragons and the fae, and come in when needed. I don't even need to call them – they just arrive when the energy is right, and our work begins then.

Last year one of my beehives became sick and I feared it would die. It did not! Unicorns came in throngs to work on it, and their love of the honey bees and their high-frequency energy healed the hive.

I feel them particularly around the winter solstice. I often see them wearing wreaths of red roses around their necks. I call them into my house when my boys aren't getting along or when as a family we are arguing too much and need some blessed energy. I have seen them come into our plane from the cosmos above and from the inner Earth plane below.

They are arriving en masse *now, as children are being born who hold their frequency and as humans in general are beginning to wake up and recognize their own divine light. We are all of the One Heart.*

PART II

UNICORNS AND HEALING

CHAPTER 19

Unicorn Healing

All angelic beings of the seventh dimension and above have
the power to heal your spiritual, mental, emotional and
physical bodies. Blockages of any kind in the physical body are
caused by unhelpful spiritual, mental and emotional patterns,
which crystallize into dis-ease. Unresolved thoughts or emotions
eventually cause a physical problem, so even the outcome of an
accident is precise and never random.

> *When the source of the mental or*
> *emotional imbalance or blockage is*
> *dissolved, the person is healed.*

For example, you may have had thoughts whirling round for a
long time about being stuck in a job where you are unfulfilled.
You may be suppressing huge amounts of resentment because
you feel unrecognized. Eventually this crystallizes into a
physical dis-ease, say varicose veins. Unicorn healing may only
touch you for a second, but in that flash your frequency rises.

You value yourself, realize you can move on to do something that is worthwhile to you and you let go of the resentment. You change your life and your attitude and the dis-ease starts to dissolve. This may be instant, in which case it is called a miracle, or gradual, in which case it is a miracle slowed down!

When the past is forgiven, released and replaced
with higher understanding, healing occurs.

During the lunch break at a seminar, a lady slipped a note onto my table. It said that she had attended one of my weekend workshops a couple of years earlier and after we had worked with unicorns, a longstanding health problem had gone. Several years later, she introduced herself to me again and said that the auto-immune problem had never recurred. It was a lovely reminder to me that just being in the presence of unicorns can heal you.

Whenever you think about unicorns, talk to others about them, write about or draw them, you are tuning in to their light. Whenever you are in the energy of these illumined beings, healing and magic can occur.

Immerse yourself in unicorn energy
and expect magic to happen.

Unicorns are beings of love and compassion, and the healing of humanity is one of their missions. As well as healing you when you are awake and in their presence, they may heal you in sleep, dreams or meditation.

A unicorn heals by taking your frequency
higher than the frequency of an illness.

Can Unicorns Always Heal You?

They can. However, they may not, because they cannot
contravene your free will. So, you must ask for the healing you
need. If we do this, unicorns will send you as much light as you
are able to accept. They will never blow your fuses.

It needn't be a formal request. People often do ask for help
without consciously realizing that they are setting spiritual
forces in motion. Just sitting wearily on your bed, rubbing your
tired eyes and thinking, *Oh God, I could do with some help with
this*, draws spiritual assistance to you.

What Happens If You Ask for Healing But It Does Not Take Place?

The only time unicorns do not send healing is if your soul says,
'No.' This happens if your Higher Self wishes you to learn from
your illness or trauma. Here are some possible reasons:

- Perhaps your soul has a contract with someone else to look
  after or heal you.

- It may be that your soul needs the trauma in order to
  strengthen you or teach you patience.

- It may want you to go through the experience for your own
  spiritual growth.

- You may need the lessons offered by a physical operation.

- There may be deeply entrenched past-life karma that still
  needs to be released.

- You may believe you don't deserve healing or that it isn't
  possible. This will block your healing.

- There may be a belief in the collective consciousness of humankind that your illness cannot be healed.

Some years ago a mother brought her son to see me. He had been severely disabled in a car accident and could no longer walk. However, she could not accept it and believed that unicorns could heal him. Well, of course they could, but when I talked to Kumeka about it, he said it would not happen because there was a very strong belief in the collective consciousness that this type of damage was beyond repair. Interestingly, rigidly held limiting beliefs like this are beginning to dissolve as the frequency of the planet and humanity in general is rising and as people open their minds to new possibilities.

If your soul insists that you experience a physical or mental dis-ease or an accident because it is the only way you will learn a spiritual lesson, unicorns must honour the dictates of your soul and step aside. However, at this time karma is surfacing to be explored and transmuted, so it is relatively rare for a soul to decline healing.

Healing Others with Unicorn Energy

Healers work in many ways, for example through massage, chanting, sound, herbs or the laying on of hands. Some are adept at bringing unicorn energy through and using it to heal others. Many people are working intuitively with unicorns and doing wonderful work.

Katie told me that she went three times to see an incredible healer from Wicklow in Ireland. In the last session the healer was overwhelmed when Katie's own personal unicorn came in and placed his horn first on her heart and then actually through it. He was vast in size and pure white. Katie wrote:

It felt so unbelievable I can't quite describe it, but my entire body shook and vibrated on a different frequency. He healed so much in my heart, and not just in this lifetime. He told me I was cleared of the suffering from this and every lifetime. He was surrounded by Pleiadians, who had also been waiting for me to ask them to help. He said that I was finally ready and he would never leave my side. I was incredibly emotional. It was just the most powerful healing.

Katie's unicorn then told her that she could use his horn whenever she needed to, but at that time just for herself. Interestingly, she had already begun to think of the people she could help through it in her job as a medical acupuncturist. Now she has permission to use unicorn healing on others. She uses a selenite wand on people before she treats them and feels this brings her unicorn in.

She added, 'At night he comes to me and sometimes my room lights up. I have asked my partner if it wakes him and it doesn't!'

Here is an exercise you can use to practise unicorn healing:

UNICORN HEALING

~ If you have a selenite wand, or even a small piece of selenite, hold it.

~ Be still and quiet, for unicorns touch you in silence.

~ Ask your unicorn to come to you.

~ Know that it is standing in front of you.

~ Think of something you wish to heal in your spiritual, mental, emotional or physical body.

~ Silently affirm that you are ready to release your ego around anything that has allowed this to develop.

~ Allow your unicorn to place his horn of light where it is most needed.

~ Relax and allow healing magic to take place.

~ Thank your unicorn.

CHAPTER 20

Unicorn Soul Healing

Most of us have had experiences on many planets, in many star systems and even in other universes. The majority of us have incarnated many times on Earth. We have all been on a long, eventful soul journey full of learning, trauma and magical moments. The challenges and traumas we have undertaken in the past have often left scars on our soul. Unicorns are stepping forward to heal them now.

When she was in her early twenties, Jennifer Simis-Rapos frequently had intense dreams and visions of a past life as Joan of Arc. In that life she had tried to bring peace, but no one had listened, and in the end she saw herself being burned at the stake. She didn't suffer, as she ascended into the light, but Archangel Michael showed her how that incarnation had affected her: as a result, in this lifetime she was very afraid of telling people that she was a psychic medium. During a Zoom workshop with Tim Whild, her unicorn gave her soul healing for her throat chakra. Afterwards she clairvoyantly saw a huge unicorn, its horn blazing pure diamond-white light, which it shone onto her. She felt it was time for her to start her life mission and that her unicorn was moving her towards it.

The source of your current challenges may, however, not be anything to do with you personally. It may originate from family or ancestral karma or even country or world karma that you have taken on, and this has to be healed at a soul level.

I was very touched and impressed by the story Alicia shared. She had received my request for people to share their unicorn stories and felt very excited. She already had a good relationship with her unicorn, Whisper, and decided this was an opportunity to connect more deeply with him. She lit a candle, played her rose quartz bowl and sang Whisper's name. He connected with her in a way that had never happened before and took her back to her pre-life decisions, her gestation time, childhood and teenage years, and then through her adult life so far. It was a magical and profound soul-healing journey.

This is the story that her unicorn revealed to her:

Three months before my birth, my mother felt a strong desire to go and see her mother. It was a three-hour bus journey to my grandmother's farm, which was an amazing and magical place. My grandmother was in perfect health and delighted to see her daughter. She was very happy and excited to show her a beautiful blanket she was making for me. A few hours later, suddenly and unexpectedly, my grandmother died. The unicorn showed me that when that happened I was asked on the higher planes if I wanted to change my destiny and be in service to humanity. I accepted without hesitation. At that moment I was enveloped by a golden Christ Light.

Three months later I was born. My mom decided to change the name she had chosen for me and baptized me with my grandmother's name.

When I was three years old my family moved from Colombia to Mexico City. I felt very at home there, but one day, quite unexpectedly, my parents decided to send me back to Colombia to live with my grandfather. I said goodbye to them and my little brother without understanding why I was being sent away.

Sometimes my grandfather took me to his farm, where my grandmother had died. When I was there I would ride a beautiful white horse with blue eyes that he gave to me. This horse was my best friend, my companion, my guide. He had something special and unique that I couldn't feel in the other horses there. He made me feel safe and that I belonged. As I grew up, I galloped on him for hours, going to the most magical places in the mountains, having long conversations with him and becoming one with him. My favourite place was a waterfall encircled by beautiful trees, where I would sit and be still with my horse. There we were surrounded by unicorns and the angelic realms.

When my family returned to my country, we went to live in another city, and the wonder and magic began to fade away. But I still remember the day my guardian angel told me that my soul had come to Earth in service to humanity.

When I got married, I began seeking for deeper answers. I learned about meditation and angels and studied many healing modalities. Years later, I got divorced and decided to move to North America. I had two children and was expecting a third. I did not know what challenging initiations were awaiting me, but I asked for help from the bottom of my heart and reconnected with the angelic realms in a deep and profound way.

Almost at once my unicorn, Whisper, arrived one Full Moon at midnight and gave me the support I needed. He became a great companion and began to heal me on a deeper level. His light is so bright and magnificent that he has helped me little by little to remember my divine essence. He has purified me, dissolving and healing the deepest and most profound wounds of my soul. He has raised my frequency and given me the strength to take the next step on my soul journey with the energy to do what I believe is right for the highest good of all. He has helped me to hold my vision and given me courage and faith to face my challenges and fulfil my soul contract.

I am sharing one of the greatest gifts I have had in this life: reconnecting with my magnificent unicorn.

She adds that with her connection to Whisper, she now has something that no one can ever take away.

Many people have told me of their beautiful connection with unicorns, as well as other beings from the angelic realms. Jennifer Simis-Rapos has always been a psychic medium and connected with spirit. When she was a child, she physically saw her guardian angel, who appeared to her as a huge white light. Now she connects closely with her unicorn as well as with archangels and dragons. She wrote:

I've always believed in unicorns and I first connected with my unicorn guide as a teen. He introduced himself to me in a dream. I was very ill at that time and was diagnosed in the hospital with aplastic anaemia and endometriosis. I almost died of a high fever and my immune system shut down. I had an operation. Then I dreamed about a beautiful unicorn who looked right at me and gave me healing. In fact, both my guardian angel and unicorn gave me healing. My unicorn guide later communicated telepathically that I would work with the unicorn realms when I was older and told me that it had been my unicorn in Atlantis.

Unicorn Soul Healing from the Brow Chakra

Soul healing happens in many ways. Like Brenda, you may not even be aware of the amazing unicorn soul-healing work you are doing. Brenda's daughters wanted a unicorn party, so she set about getting in all the supplies. She explained:

I had no clue about the beauty of the wondrous beings, but at the end of my sessions as a massage therapist I always get a bright light in my brow chakra, which I aim at my clients for healing. The light is always so bright that I feel as though I am looking at the sun. I have never known what this is, but have just continued to use it for healing at the end of each session.

As I was shopping for the party, I came across my first unicorn book and was struck by the words: 'Their horn can be likened to a magic wand pouring out divine energy. Whenever they direct this light, healing takes place. This is not just physical and emotional healing, but also soul healing.'

At that moment I really saw the connection between the light in my brow chakra and unicorns. I loved this because I had been calling on Archangel Michael to heal the souls of my clients and directing a light into their brow chakra. The Wonder of Unicorns *confirmed all I had been doing for my clients! After reading the unicorn book, I now have more wisdom about what*

I am connecting to. Excited to have connected with the magic of unicorns!

Here is a unicorn soul-healing visualization you can do for someone. It doesn't matter whether they are present or absent, the steps are the same. In either case, you must, however, ask them for permission first. If this is not physically possible, mentally ask their Higher Self for consent and have a clear sense that they agree to the healing before proceeding.

SOUL HEALING WITH UNICORNS

~ Set your intention to offer soul healing to someone, and imagine that person in front of you.

~ Call in your unicorn and sense both of you being in a cocoon of pure white light.

~ Breathe the white light into yourself, then feel it gathering in your third eye.

~ Be aware of the other person's soul journey stretching out from their third eye into the universe. You may receive pictures of or sense a lower vibration in parts of their soul journey.

~ Let white light pour out of your third eye to touch and illuminate their soul journey wherever needed.

~ See their past pathway light up with white fire.

~ When you feel the healing is finished, close their soul pathway.

~ Mentally separate yourself from the person you've been working with.

~ Thank your unicorn and open your eyes.

~ It can be really helpful for both of you to share what you experienced and discuss what it means to you.

CHAPTER 21

Unicorns Heal Your
Inner Child

U nicorns love children because of their innocence. This also applies to the inner child. Unicorns love that part of you!

Many illnesses have their origin in the hurt, fear or anger of the inner child, for however loving and devoted the parents, no baby or child can receive all the love, understanding or support it needs. A fragile baby interprets its surroundings and its parents' actions through the eyes of its vulnerability and also through the lenses of its past-life experiences. Also, most humans are very adept at putting themselves and one another down, often out of habit, and this is very frightening or humiliating for a youngster. These impressions can lie deep in your consciousness and healing them all with love and understanding is part of your journey.

When Ursula Boeckl read *The Wonder of Unicorns*, it inspired her to connect with unicorns and Pegasi and do energy work. In a special place in nature that felt very magical to her, she called to them. She wrote:

I felt their presence and could see them with my inner eye. I was usually aware of adult ones and sometimes also a unicorn or Pegasus foal. I just love their peaceful loving energy. It is so soothing, comforting and blissful and fun. I then started to work with the Pegasi and unicorns to heal and comfort my inner child. I urgently needed emotional comfort, so I called for a Pegasus and leaned my inner child against it. That helped a little, yet I felt more support was needed. Then I was invited by the Pegasus to climb onto his back and lie between his wings. I did so and found that there I could let go completely. We flew together for a while through the sky. I felt totally safe and was fully supported by his strength and deep love. It was such an intimate, unconditional, love-filled connection that I did heal on a deep level.

Any healing that you can do in your inner world, you can do in your physical life. This is why visualization is so powerful and effective.

Unicorns can add energy to your visualizations.

In the following visualization, your unicorn will assist you to heal your inner child. So much of your buried hurt, guilt and anger may still be held in that vulnerable part of you. Every time you think you aren't good enough, or worthy or good-looking or clever, your inner child shrivels a little. And even if your outer self appears over confident, brash or bullying, this is a cover-up for the insecure inner self.

Your wise adult self can parent your child to encourage and help it. However, when you ask unicorns, who carry pure Divine Feminine love, to heal your inner child, a much deeper transformation takes place.

Journey with Your Unicorn to Heal Your Inner Child

~ Find a place where you can relax and be undisturbed.

~ Close your eyes and sense that you are surrounded by a very soft, pure white cloud.

~ You find yourself preparing to set off on a healing journey.

~ As you take your first step, your unicorn appears beside you and you know that miracles can happen.

~ You progress along the path and see a house ahead of you. This house may be familiar or you may not recognize it. Is it large or small?

~ Your unicorn waits patiently while you enter the house and explore.

~ You find that there is a room with its door firmly closed. It may just be shut or it may be locked or even padlocked.

~ If you need a key, your unicorn will give you the right one. Notice what it is like. Is it large or small, plain or ornate, brass, iron or golden?

~ It is time to open the door. Before you enter the room, be quietly receptive as your unicorn places a ball of pure white compassion in your heart chakra. Accept it fully and feel it.

~ Your inner child is in the room, waiting for you. It needs healing. Is it afraid, angry, hurt or ready to be manipulative?

~ Hug your child. Listen to it. Tell it you love it.

~ Take your child into the sunshine to play.

~ When it is smiling and happy, your unicorn pours a stream of healing white love into its heart.

~   Take your inner child into your heart chakra.

~   Let your unicorn hold you both in a beautiful white healing cocoon.

~   Thank your unicorn and be prepared to have kinder, more supportive thoughts about yourself.

INTERPRETATION

The house represents your consciousness. So, if it was familiar, this suggests you may well recognize the feelings of the inner child or alternatively that something from that time has left a meaningful impression on you. If you did not recognize the house, perhaps you are unaware of the feelings you are burying.

If the house was large, it infers that this is quite a big thing for you to deal with, so it is very important to heal that aspect of your inner child.

The room with a shut door represents a hidden part of you.

Was it just shut? This indicates that the hurt was not acknowledged, but you are ready to access it.

Was it locked? This suggests that you did not want to look at it.

Was it padlocked? You really have buried it, so it is important to receive unicorn healing.

The key is your way of accessing your hurting aspect.

If it was small, this is something you are ready to engage in.

If it was large, this is a big thing for you to unlock, so treat yourself with respect.

A golden key suggests that a very wise and special part of you needs to access your inner child with care.

An iron key indicates that your inner child is robust enough to accept your help.

A delicate filigree key warns that you need to be careful and tactful in the way you handle your inner child.

Healing the Inner Child of Humanity

A child who feels deeply loved, accepted and worthwhile automatically grows up to spread peace, joy and comfort and empower others. But throughout the world there are people who are hurting at the level of the inner child. Inside every terrorist or dictator or sociopath there is an angry, hurt toddler longing for validation and love.

Some souls come into the most challenging conditions of war, poverty or even starvation, and they certainly have feelings about it on an inner child level. Others are orphans experiencing abandonment. In addition, no parent is perfect, however good their intentions and however hard they try! A toddler may have loving parents who are doing their best, but the seed for a hurt inner child is still sown. This is because it lies within the individual. One baby may feel bereft and abandoned if its mother does not pick it up as soon as it wakes. Another is content to gurgle and relax as it waits for attention. One feels acute jealousy or a sense of injustice if a sibling has more attention. Another accepts it with an open heart.

However it feels, right from the moment of birth the thoughts and reactions of the baby are influencing its DNA, building up a life of distress and conflict or happiness and health.

Unicorns can only touch those whose frequency is high enough. To him that hath shall be given. But even in the most dreadful conditions some souls are able to take inner decisions that lead to forgiveness and acceptance. As soon as they do so, unicorn energy is able to help them.

To heal the inner child of the whole of humanity, the frequency of the world has to rise. Every single prayer you send out for the planet makes a difference, for angels respond. The prayer may only last for a fraction of a second, but it will open the way for unicorn energy to touch those in greatest need.

HEALING THE INNER CHILD OF HUMANITY

~ Find a place where you can be quiet and undisturbed.

~ Close your eyes and take a few moments to breathe in a calm, relaxed way.

~ Your unicorn appears beside you, knowing that you have a mission to accomplish.

~ Thank it for coming to you and then find yourself on its back.

~ As it rises in the air, tell it that you are asking the unicorns to heal the inner child of all of humanity.

~ It acknowledges the enormity of this mission with a twitch of its ears.

~ Together you fly above the world.

~ Have a sense of the billions of people on Earth – some happy and fulfilled, many hurting in some way.

~ See the hurting masses as small children, eyes closed, crying out for assistance and compassion.

~ Mentally say: 'I now call on the angelic realms to raise the frequency of the world so that unicorns can touch the inner child of each individual.'

~ See Angel Mary placing aquamarine columns of light reaching from Heaven to Earth throughout the world. These radiate a beautiful compassionate and caring energy.

~ Then Archangel Michael places deep blue columns of light into the heart of war zones, bringing strength to the people there.

~ Archangel Chamuel now adds glorious pink columns of light and these radiate hope-filled love.

~ Then everywhere you can see columns of pure archangel light streaming down to Earth.

~ Archangel Gabriel's white light brings purification.

~ Archangel Jophiel's pale yellow light brings wisdom.

~ Archangel Raphael's emerald green light spreads healing and enlightenment.

~ You may see many other columns of light spanning the dimensions between Heaven and Earth.

~ There is a clap of thunder and a flash of light as each of these columns of light switches to a higher frequency.

~ For an instant the billions of children open their eyes and see the light.

~ Millions of unicorns float above the world, pouring out pure white light. It is a spectacular sight.

~ Pure white Source love touches the heart and soul of every receptive child.

~ Sense a heartbeat of peace and gratitude throughout the world.

~ And as quickly as they have turned them on, the archangels withdraw the columns into the heavenly realms.

~ Let the love, peace, strength and wisdom that have touched the world soak into you as you rest on your unicorn.

~ And then your beloved unicorn quietly and slowly floats back to Earth with you.

~ Dismount and stroke it as you thank it.

~ Open your eyes.

CHAPTER 22

Unicorns Heal Ancestral Beliefs and Issues

You are influenced by your ancestors going back seven generations. All the restrictive thoughts that come from the beliefs of your parents, grandparents and great-grandparents reaching back for centuries are landing in your life now. Not only that – if you had aunts and uncles and great-aunts and great-uncles during that period who had no children, then you, along with your siblings and cousins, will take on their unresolved beliefs. If you are an only child, the buck rests with you. If for some reason you don't accept it, your cousins will share it between them. If you were adopted, you will still carry the beliefs of your blood ancestry. And you may also be dealing with those of your adoptive family.

Some people have made valiant soul choices and have incarnated with a huge challenge to face. Many of these individuals have taken a physical body in a particular family again and again and are very familiar with its energies, though this does not lessen the challenge. Others have viewed the situation from the spiritual world before birth, and even though their family is unfamiliar at a soul level, have decided they are strong enough to deal with it. Interestingly, some IVF children, who have the capacity to view challenges from a new and fresh angle, are able to heal whole families.

Healing Ancestral Beliefs

Imagine a family where there is a deeply held conviction that the eldest son must follow in his father's footsteps and take over the family business or become a dustman or a barrister. If a soul incarnates as that eldest son with a soul urge to be a musician, expressing his soul mission will require determination, courage, possibly the readiness to let go of his family and many other qualities. If he surrenders to the family pattern, his true light will never shine and he will not fulfil his destiny.

I was told by a spiritual reader that one of my grandfathers, who died before I was born, had the belief that everyone else had to come first. This belief had never been dissolved and no one else had taken it on, so my soul had accepted it, but the reader said it was holding back my ascension. My first reaction was that this was not correct, but the very next day a friend came to lunch. He was suggesting a project and wanted me to present it to someone. Then he added, 'But I know you. You'll ask all about him and then you won't have time to talk about the project.' Suddenly it clicked. These patterns manifest in many ways.

After that, I started to notice how my grandfather's belief was affecting me and asked unicorns to help me release it. Within a week I had decided to move to a location where I felt freer to be myself!

Recognizing Beliefs

How can you spot ancestral beliefs and patterns? Watch your words and thoughts constantly. Here are some examples of beliefs that may cross your mind or tumble from your lips, and there are hundreds of others:

- 'It's not fair, no one understands me/listens to me/believes me/appreciates me/loves me.'

- 'I never get what I want/deserve/need.'

- 'I've got to get away, take time for myself.'

- 'I'll never be free. I feel suffocated.'

- 'It's too late.'

They may not all be like this. You may well have life-affirming, happy, successful beliefs that you have inherited from your ancestral lines. Be grateful and enjoy them.

Help from Unicorns

Some individuals are presented with challenges at the beginning of their life, others in the middle and others at the end. Some brave ones have initiations all through their incarnation. Sometimes you're not even aware of a test, you just have a feeling of constriction or lack of freedom or of being controlled. If you realize that you've given away your freedom to be yourself, ask unicorns to help. They will work with Archangel Michael to enable you to stand up for yourself and speak your truth.

Sometimes your challenges result in you feeling depressed or without hope, unworthy or unable to achieve your visions. Again, if you feel like this, ask unicorns for help. They will work with Archangel Uriel to assist you. They can help you slough off ancient guilt.

Beliefs can be a tangle of prickly energies. They can stultify, hurt or block you. When you set yourself free from them, you can fly.

Here is a visualization to take you on a journey with unicorns that will help you clear the tangle of unhelpful ancestral beliefs you may be carrying. Each time you do this, you will shift something in your unconscious mind.

UNICORNS HELPING YOU TO UNTANGLE AND CLEAR UNHELPFUL ANCESTRAL BELIEFS

Before you start, think about some of the challenges you have experienced. As you contemplate these and their ramifications in your life, notice the thoughts you are having and write them down. This is very important.

~ Find a place where you can be quiet and undisturbed.

~ Close your eyes and ask your unicorn to come to you.

~ When you see or sense it arrive, greet it with love and reverence.

~ Say, 'Beloved unicorn, please dissolve the ancestral beliefs that are holding me back. I am ready to release them.'

~ Your unicorn looks at you and nods, then invites you to ride with him.

~ Together you fly to a huge mountain and land on the slope.

~ Ahead of you is a thicket of brambles and thorns. They represent the unwanted ancestral beliefs you are holding in your consciousness.

~ Your unicorn presents you with whatever you need to clear the thicket, or at least make a path through it.

~ Is the thicket large or small? Does it feel easy to clear or difficult? Is it thorny? Are there dead branches to move away? Are there creatures hiding in it?

~ Take your time and do whatever you need to do to clear away your blockages.

~ When you have finished, your unicorn touches your forehead with its horn of light and pours healing white light into your mind.

~ Relax and sense diamond-white light flashing in your mental body as the unicorn energy dissolves unhelpful ancestral beliefs.

~ And now your unicorn takes you higher up the mountain.

~ Ahead you see a beautiful waterfall cascading like a bridal veil.

~ Without pausing, your unicorn takes you right through it and you find yourself in the most beautiful sun-filled garden, full of luscious fruit and beautiful flowers.

~ Your unicorn tells you that when you accept all the wonderful, life-affirming, soul-satisfying beliefs of your ancestors, your life will be filled with a cornucopia of delight.

~ Enjoy the garden.

~ Your unicorn brings you back through the waterfall and down the mountain, through the place where the thicket was, to where you started from.

~ Know that your journey with your unicorn has lit up something within you.

Healing Unresolved Family and Ancestral Issues

Energies of all kinds are passed down through families. If one of your ancestors was, for example, in a religious order and took a vow that they did not rescind, the energy of the vow will be passed down your family line. If they had children, one or more of them will have undertaken to carry it on. If there were no children, it will go to nephews and nieces. These agreements are made at a spiritual level without our conscious participation or knowledge.

Wonderful gifts and qualities can pass down the family line. Perhaps a great-great-grandmother was a talented flautist and long after she is dead a child in a later generation carries the gift.

> *You can call on unicorns to light up*
> *ancestral gifts to activate them for you.*

It may also be, for example, that an unmarried aunt is an incredibly kind and caring person. After she dies, it is noticed that one of her nieces is very like her. This is often because the qualities the aunt developed pass on to the relation.

With these serendipities, no healing is called for, but some energetic legacies are more problematic:

- If a relative up to seven generations back was in debt and died without repaying it, the karma of it continues through the family line and family members may find themselves suddenly losing a lot of money.

- Alcoholism, drug addiction or any form of obsession that is unresolved often emerges generations later. People may sigh,

'Jack's a heavy drinker, just like his great-grandfather.' In fact he is carrying that ancestral cloud.

- A person may commit suicide because they hear the call to return to the spiritual realms. However, it may be a way to opt out of dealing with a situation instead. In the latter case, someone down the line will have to deal with it in their stead.

All these and many other unresolved ancestral issues are like heavy bricks. They may be nothing to do with you, yet you have to carry them, either because your soul has nobly volunteered or because you are obliged to do so when family karmic debts are called in.

In the past people were able to sidestep the unresolved issues of their deceased relatives. Now this is no longer possible, because the new Golden Age starts in 2032 and all karma must be cleared by then. Unresolved family and ancestral issues are knocking at our doors in a way that can no longer be ignored.

Many people now are carrying heavy
rucksacks of ancestral unfinished business,
but unicorns are ready to lighten the load.

LIGHTENING YOUR ANCESTRAL LOAD

~ Find a place where you can be quiet and undisturbed.

~ Close your eyes and relax.

~ On each out-breath, feel a soft white light flowing with your breath round your body until you are enveloped in a ball of white light.

~ Be aware of your unicorn standing by you, waiting to help you.

~ As you stroke it, tell it that you wish to lighten the load of ancestral bricks you are carrying and ask it please to help you.

~ A rucksack appears in front of you. Is it big, small, heavy or light?

~ You pick it up and notice the dead energy. Look inside it. How many bricks are in it? Place it on your back. How does it feel? Is it familiar?

~ Climb onto your beloved unicorn's back and feel the love and the safety it offers.

~ Your unicorn is walking slowly with you up a dark, narrow, stony valley.

~ The rocks seem very close, as if they are about to squeeze you. You may have a sense of constriction and control. You cannot escape from this tight space without shifting some of the rocks.

~ All the tools you need to clear the path are available to you and you get down from your unicorn and do what needs to be done.

~ When the path is totally clear, you place your rucksack in front of your unicorn.

~ Tell it you have done clearance work and ask it under grace to transmute the energy of those bricks.

~ Your unicorn pours pure Source love over and into the rucksack until it totally disappears.

~ You breathe deeply, realizing that unconsciously you have cleared ancestral blocks.

~ Notice how you feel.

~ Archangel Michael appears before you. Feel his wonderful light.

~ He places a dark blue ball of truth into your throat and tells you that the truth has set you free.

~   He commands that you now stand up for yourself. Speak your truth.

~   See yourself doing this. Take your time to say what you need to say.

~   Now your unicorn lovingly pours a shimmering cascade of blessings over you, lighting up any ancestral gifts you are ready to bring into your life.

~   Take your time to experience the joy of this.

~   Smile as you see that the narrow gorge has opened out into a wider vista.

~   Expect new opportunities and miracles as you find yourself back where you started from, knowing that something has shifted in your consciousness.

~   Thank your unicorn and Archangel Michael.

CHAPTER 23

Unicorns Take Your Soul Desires to Source

True soul satisfaction is one of the greatest gifts you can have in your lifetime. When you feel totally fulfilled, your daily life is one of contentment and problems become insignificant. Everything falls into perspective. One of the most beautiful offerings that unicorns present to you is the chance to have your soul desires taken to Source for a blessing.

This is so powerful that they usually take your request to the masters of the Himalayas first. This raises its vibration so that the unicorns can carry it to the Seraphim, who hand it to Source. Then miracles can happen.

So here is a little information about the masters of the Himalayas as well as the Seraphim.

The Masters of the Himalayas

The Himalayas are still the purest place on the planet. Above their snow-capped peaks, the masters of the Himalayas have their etheric retreat. There are 12 masters, all wise ancient beings who hold the light of the mountains as well as much wisdom for the planet, and their retreat is a space of incredible beauty, purity and light.

In this range the land itself is rich in ancient wisdom. Most importantly, all sentient beings, including mountains, emit notes, and the song of the Himalayas contains the melodies of the crystals, minerals and gems embedded there. The masters oversee all this and hold this pure light steady for the world.

Unicorns often bring lower energy that has been released anywhere in the planet to the Himalayas for purification, though they can take 'stuff' to other parts of the universe for transmutation too.

If you are visiting the Intergalactic Council with a petition to help yourself or the world, unicorns sometimes take you to this special retreat first, so that you can receive guidance and wisdom from the masters and boost your light before approaching the Council.

The Seraphim

The Seraphim are pure white 12th-dimensional angelic beings. They surround the Godhead and sing the visions of Source into manifestation. For example, when Source envisioned the original concept for Earth, the Seraphim focused on it while chanting 'Om'. This projected the image into the universe so that it could gather the energy needed to create it. Then other angels and dragons brought the planet into physical reality.

Two of the mighty Seraphim are currently working with humanity. These are Seraphina and Seraphiel. Unicorns co-operate with them for our highest good.

What Brings You Soul Satisfaction?

Whatever gives you joy, peace, contentment or deep pleasure brings you soul satisfaction. It may be creative or artistic work, or a particular vocation, like being a health professional or a teacher. Many people find peace and contentment when they are out in nature with trees and birds. Others find it by the ocean. For some, their greatest satisfaction is in challenging their physical body in sport. You may want to be an inventor or even to create a business with integrity.

People often ask me, 'What is my soul mission?' The answer is always: 'It is what gives you joy and satisfaction.'

Sometimes someone thinks they cannot fulfil their soul mission. They say that they would love to be a painter, for example, but they cannot do that because they have to support their family. Or they have always wanted to travel, but never been able to. Well, unicorns make magic happen.

CO-OPERATING WITH UNICORNS TO TAKE YOUR SOUL DESIRES TO SOURCE

PREPARATION

~   Give yourself time to decide what you really want. This is not something that feeds your ego, or even makes your heart rejoice, it is something that gives you a true sense of fulfilment.

~   Write it down. Committing your soul desires to paper is a significant step towards bringing them to fruition.

~   Light a candle to raise the frequency.

~   Find a place where you can be quiet and undisturbed.

VISUALIZATION TO TAKE YOUR SOUL DESIRES TO THE MASTERS OF THE HIMALAYAS

~ Close your eyes and breathe comfortably until you feel relaxed.

~ Picture yourself in a rich and verdant valley, where birds are singing and waterfalls are cascading over rocks. Notice how blue the sky is and how golden the sun. It is so peaceful and still here.

~ Mentally call your unicorn and instantly see it standing in front of you, a pure shimmering white horse emanating love, peace and white light.

~ Feel its love enfolding you.

~ Whisper to it all the desires of your soul.

~ Notice how patiently it waits for you to finish.

~ When you have done so, ask it to help you fulfil those desires.

~ It nods solemnly and invites you to sit on its back.

~ You rise, safe and relaxed, higher and higher in a column of light. You are above the valley. You are above mountain peaks.

~ The glorious etheric temples of the masters of the Himalayas lie ahead.

~ The unicorn flies with you through 12 pillars of white flame into a central courtyard.

~ Here the 12 masters await you. They greet you with their hands in *Namaste*, the prayer position.

~ You hand them the list of soul desires that you have written.

~ One of them takes it and holds it, while they all pour light into it until it becomes a blazing diamond.

~ The master returns the diamond to you and you accept it with a bow of your head.

Taking your Soul Desires through the Seraphim to Source

~ The unicorn tells you that it is time for the last stage of your mission. You are to ask the Seraphim to take your request to Source for a blessing.

~ Your move back through the 12 pillars of white flame and float together into the higher dimensions.

~ Be aware of ineffable Seraphim surrounding the White Fire of the Godhead. You may even hear them singing.

~ The unicorn gently approaches Seraphiel, one of the Seraphim, who is illuminated with rainbow lights.

~ You humbly hand him your blazing diamond, the illumined energy of your soul desires, and ask him to take it to Source for a blessing.

~ Seraphiel takes it and disappears into the White Fire of the Godhead.

~ You wait patiently and at last he returns.

~ He hands you back the diamond. What does it look like? Is it bigger, brighter, a different colour? Or is it something else entirely?

~ As the unicorn glides peacefully back with you, take some time to consider what the blessing means for your life.

~ And then you arrive back where you started from. Thank the unicorn and open your eyes.

CHAPTER 24

Unicorns Remove the Veils of Illusion

Every soul who comes to Earth must go through the Veil of Amnesia. This consists of the Seven Veils of Illusion. As each one dissolves, you become more enlightened. When they have all dissolved, you achieve total enlightenment. Unicorns are the angelic beings that can help you with this quest.

The chaos and turbulence of the world are third-dimensional drama. It may be horrible to watch and even worse to go through, but it is exciting, and this is why much of humanity is still attached to it. All that pain, hurt, jealousy, anger or love is highly addictive, and while you have a part in the play, you feel alive – unhappy or scared maybe, but definitely alive. Everyone involved in any form of drama is signing up for it. It is a possible third-dimensional experience and it is a choice. However, this turbulent energy clouds who you truly are and makes it difficult for unicorns to reach you. If you are caught up in a less than desirable human production, whether it is family conflict, economic problems, war or political upheaval, unicorns cannot even see you. So, if you are in such a situation, stop engaging in it, for this adds energy to it. Quit judging all sides. Centre yourself. Look at everything from a higher perspective and bring yourself into harmony. Then your light will shine clearly and unicorns will be able to see you, approach you and transform your life.

If you are in the middle of a dark story, you may find this impossible to believe, for the more intense the challenge, the harder the test. However, even in desperate situations, there are those who stay calm, centred and non-judgemental. They witness what is happening without engaging in it. This is enlightenment consciousness and these people's light becomes very pure.

The best way to help yourself and the world is to maintain harmony and rise above what is happening. The divine plan is working out, so trust in it. Focus on love and Oneness and a unicorn may appear in your life to help you take the next step. This will eventually move you away from the scenario altogether to live life from another perspective.

The Seven Veils of Illusion

The seven Veils of Illusion shroud your third eye on Earth and as a result you forget your soul journey and who you truly are. You may have partially dissolved some or even most of them during this and other lifetimes, but you must remove them fully to reach the pinnacle of enlightenment. Unicorns have said that if you look at a unicorn Orb for a while, asking for these veils to be removed, they will work with you to release a greater part of one of them, or even draw one back entirely. This accelerates your ascension as well as your enlightenment and enables you to see life from a divine perspective.

The Seventh Veil

The Seventh Veil is red and is the furthest away from the third eye. It is the first to be removed when you wake up at a soul level and take responsibility for creating or attracting every single thing in your life. As this veil thins, you no longer blame another person for your situation, but instead ask, 'How did I create or attract this circumstance?' If you ask unicorns, they will help reveal the answer to you. In this way, they help you along your path to mastery.

Affirmation:
*'I am totally responsible for attracting or
creating every single circumstance in my life.'*

The Sixth Veil

The Sixth Veil is yellow, and this dissolves as you start to believe in the spirit world and trust the invisible realms to look after you and support you. Here is an example: your wedding ring is lost and your first thought is to call on Archangel Michael to ask him to look after it. You absolutely trust he is doing so and you completely cease to worry about your ring. In other words, you hand it over so that Archangel Michael can do as you requested. Then this veil is removed. This is a physical world, of course, so you also take action to find your ring. But you know Archangel Michael will have kept it safe for you.

Affirmation:
*'I totally trust the spiritual
realms to look after me.'*

The Fifth Veil

The Fifth Veil is a beautiful pink and it dissolves as you start to express unconditional love. This veil is intimately connected with your heart centre. The more you choose love as a response, the more this veil melts and the more your unicorn can connect with you.

Affirmation:
'There is only love. We are One.'

The Fourth Veil

The Fourth Veil is a radiant green and is connected to the natural world. So it is when you start to understand, respect and honour the animal world that this veil begins to lift. When you honour all of nature as well as the elemental kingdom, it is removed completely. Whenever you hug trees, bless and thank them or mentally bathe them in higher ascension energies, this veil is drawn back. Remember, when you eat delicious vegetables or see colourful flowers, to thank the elementals for their part in bringing them to fruition. As you do so, unicorns will come closer to you.

Affirmation:
'I love and thank all of nature.'

The Third Veil

As you live more and more in the angelic realms, working with angels, unicorns and dragons, the Third Veil, which is light blue, dissolves. So, think about these wondrous celestial beings often as you go about your day. Thank them for helping you. Call on them to help or bless people or situations and you will receive the blessings of the unicorn kingdom.

Affirmation:
'I act like an angel.'

The Second Veil

When you fully understand that all is connected, the Second Veil, which is deep blue, lifts. You look at the stars and know we are all an intimate and integrated part of the vast universe. You see people of different religions, cultures and colours and know all are One. When you look for the light of people's souls, more of the wonder of the universe is revealed to you and unicorns light up your third eye.

Affirmation:
'I am One with All That Is.'

The First Veil

The First Veil, which is shimmering violet, lifts when you ascend to the seventh dimension. Since 2012, we have been able to access this frequency for the first time and partially dissolve this final veil, with the help of unicorns. They can take you there, especially in meditation, though only for moments. But when you ascend or merge with your mighty I AM Presence, you become pure white light, like the unicorns themselves.

Affirmation:
'I merge with the angelic realms.'

CHAPTER 25

Unicorns and Christ Light

Unicorns carry wonderful Christ Light, which is pure Source love. It pours from Source at a 12th-dimensional frequency as an ineffable diamond-white light. It is then stepped down through white-gold and golden vibrations until it reaches a level that we can access. Currently the highest frequency of Christ Light that we can access on Earth bathes us at a ninth-dimensional level, where it is golden-white. It is stored at this frequency in Lakumay, the ascended ninth-dimensional aspect of Sirius, in a golden tetrahedron. This is surrounded by a complete rainbow.

On Earth, as soon as you open your fifth-dimensional chakras, you can be touched by the Golden Ray of Source Love carrying Christ Light. Many angels work on this golden Christ Ray, and they enfold you in it when you are ready.

A golden cloak of Christ Light is a wonderful shield, for Christ Light transmutes any lower energies that try to impact on you. Christ Light also heals at a cellular level. When you carry it, your heart lights up and at the same time ignites the hearts of others. It is a feminine energy that expands your consciousness, so that you open up to an enlightened perspective of the universe. It also lights up the keys and codes of knowledge, wisdom and spiritual technology that lie dormant in your energy fields.

Christ Light cannot vibrate at a frequency lower than the fifth dimension, but it is a perfect energy for those stepping onto the ascension path. It starts to open you up to unconditional love at a true cellular level and prepares you to access angelic energies.

Angels and unicorns will always touch you with the highest vibration you can cope with. Trust this. They always act for your highest good.

Animals Who Carry Christ Light

White animals, including those who are albino, carry some Christ Light in their souls. They are looked after by Archangel Gabriel, as well as by unicorns. Unicorns are connected to all the creatures who carry Christ Light.

In our current times, sacred animals with white fur and blue eyes are being born all over the world. These include white buffalo, lions, stags and others. These special ones bring in Christ Light and blaze it out to spread unconditional love throughout the world.

White birds, such as the gracious, elegant swan, also hold Christ Light and are kept pure by the water they swim on.

Dragons Who Carry Christ Light

Water dragons leave a trail of Christ Light wherever they float, including inside your physical body! Golden Christed Dragons, among others, spread this light. Unicorns are always close, linked to them by the Christ energy.

Names

Archangel Christine, the twin flame of Archangel Uriel, radiates a high intensity of Christ Light, as does Archangel Christiel, who oversees the unicorn kingdom.

When the word 'Christ' appears in a person's name, that person carries that energy at a soul level. So, if you have a name like Christine, Christian, Christopher or another with the Christ vibration, every time your name is spoken, it draws Christ Light to you. This automatically attracts unicorn energy too.

Your Higher Self chose your forename before you were born and imparted it telepathically to your mother.

Pools of Christ Light

Unicorns love to take you to Sirius and Lakumay, its ascended aspect, to bathe in the pools of Christ Light that are available there. In the following visualization, they will take you first to the fifth-dimensional golden pool. As you absorb the energies at a deep level, your cells will open up, as well as your heart. Then they will take you to the seventh-dimensional pool. As you relax there, you may find your potential and possibilities expand. This will enable you to accept ninth-dimensional light. If you aren't ready for it, though, the unicorns will tone down the energy to one that you can accept.

VISUALIZATION TO BATHE IN THE POOLS OF CHRIST LIGHT ON SIRIUS AND LAKUMAY

This is a really good visualization to do just before you go to sleep. Remember you don't need to follow every step exactly. Read it through and have a general idea of the journey, then take yourself through it.

~ See yourself sitting by a peaceful lake on a warm, clear, starlit night.

~ Breathe in the fragrant air.

~ As you wait there quietly, a bright white light appears in the distance and comes slowly nearer.

~ And then a magnificent shimmering white unicorn steps out of the light and stands in front of you.

~ It blesses you with a stream of love and light.

~ You reach up and touch the being of love.

~ When you have made your connection, the unicorn invites you to sit on it so that it can take you to Sirius and Lakumay.

~ You float in serenity and tranquillity through the cosmos until you reach Sirius.

~ Your unicorn takes you through a green-and-gold door to Lakumay.

BATHE IN THE FIFTH-DIMENSIONAL POOL OF CHRIST LIGHT

~ In front of you is a wonderful pool, filled with sparkling golden fifth-dimensional Christ Light. It is surrounded by colourful cascades of flowers.

~ You get off your unicorn and slip into the waters of unconditional love.

~ Rest, relax and absorb the love for as long as you wish.

~ When you step out again, many varieties of gentle white animals surround you and greet you lovingly.

~ Your heart bursts with love and peace.

BATHE IN THE SEVENTH-DIMENSIONAL POOL OF CHRIST LIGHT

~ Your unicorn takes you up along a path with blazing flares on either side.

~ At the end of the path is an archway shimmering like a golden rainbow.

~ As you pass through it, you see the golden-white seventh-dimensional pool of Christ Light, surrounded by golden flowers with rainbow auras.

~ You climb off your unicorn and merge with the Christ Light in the pool.

~ As you rest, you are aware of flashes of light. You can hear a choir of angels singing.

~ When you have absorbed all you are ready for, you find yourself on your unicorn's back again.

BATHE IN THE NINTH-DIMENSIONAL POOL OF CHRIST LIGHT

~ Now the energy has changed completely. The light from your unicorn twinkles like diamonds.

~ The great gates ahead to the ninth dimension are too bright to see, as they shimmer glittering white.

~ Your unicorn takes you through them and you stand in front of the sparkling white-gold light of the ninth-dimensional pool of Christ Light.

~ Even before you enter, you can feel the energy entering you at a cellular level.

~ You relax in the effervescent, glistening waters of life-transforming higher love.

~ Angels sing, 'There is only love.' And you feel this in your essence.

~ Spend as long as you like absorbing the love.

~ Then your unicorn brings you back to the place you started from.

~ Thank your unicorn.

When you have done this visualization a number of times, you may feel ready to go directly to the seventh-dimensional pool of Christ Light, or even to the ninth-dimensional one.

PART III

UNICORNS, GEMS AND CRYSTALS

CHAPTER 26

Unicorns and Archangel Gems

Unicorns work with archangels and they can merge their energy to illuminate people and areas. They particularly love to place their light in archangel gems to give you very high frequencies. You can then send these incredible cosmic gems lit up by unicorns to help places and situations.

Pharaohs, kings and people of rank used to wear sapphires, diamonds, rubies, emeralds and pearls purposefully, and when they were worn with pure intent, the gems would link the individual to archangels so that they could tune in to them and make wise decisions. They also gave them the charisma and power to take appropriate action.

Each jewel carries the concentrated light of an archangel and vibrates on a specific colour ray. This is why couples in love often pledge their troth with a gemstone ring. When unicorn light is added to it, or to any gemstone, the frequency rises and magic and miracles can occur.

Etheric Archangel Gems

While physical gems are potent, etheric ones hold the archangel qualities at an even higher frequency. As the angelic colour ray rises in frequency, the hue becomes more transparent, until it is almost clear with just a hint of the archangel tint in it:

- A sapphire becomes the palest translucent shimmering white-blue.

- An emerald becomes the palest translucent shimmering white-green.

- A ruby becomes the palest translucent shimmering white with a hint of red and gold.

- A diamond becomes transparent sparkling white.

- A pearl becomes a soft transparent silver-cream, glowing with pastel hues.

Valuable gems are fashioned with beautiful clear-cut facets. These are also present in etheric jewels, apart from pearls, and they cut away lower energies that no longer serve you.

Etheric Cosmic Archangel and Unicorn Gems

When a unicorn adds its light and purity to an etheric archangel gem, its power is increased tenfold and its energy is exceptionally potent and magnificent. It can only be used for the highest good, for the unicorn energy withdraws if the intention is not totally pure. An etheric cosmic archangel and unicorn gem cannot burn a person out, for it will simply not touch anyone who is not ready to receive its light. There are many people on the planet whose frequency is not yet high enough to accept this gift. However, if you create such a gem with a pure intention, it is never a waste of your time and energy, for the gem will enter the pool of cosmic light and add to it. Then, when someone is of the right frequency and asks for help, they can draw beautiful light and assistance from this pool.

CREATING AN ARCHANGEL AND UNICORN GEM

~ Imagine an enormous ethereal ninth-dimensional jewel – a cosmic sapphire, emerald, ruby, diamond or pearl. It is a vast translucent shimmering cosmic gem of unimaginable beauty.

~ Making sure your intention is totally pure, mentally call a unicorn and ask it to enter and activate the cosmic gem.

~ Be aware of a pure white unicorn touching the gem with its horn of light.

~ Then watch as the gem lights up and glows as its precious facets catch the light of the universe:

  – A ninth-dimensional cosmic sapphire lit by a unicorn is a transparent, translucent white-blue.

  – A ninth-dimensional cosmic emerald lit by a unicorn is a transparent, translucent white-green.

  – A ninth-dimensional cosmic ruby lit by a unicorn is a transparent, translucent white pink and gold.

  – A ninth-dimensional cosmic diamond lit by a unicorn is a transparent, translucent white.

  – A ninth-dimensional cosmic pearl lit by a unicorn is a glowing transparent silver-cream.

How to Use Ninth-Dimensional Cosmic Archangel and Unicorn Gems

SENDING ILLUMINED GRACE

When you wish to serve, you can make a huge difference to the planet, even when you are sitting calmly at home, by sending illumined grace to a person, place or situation. You can also do this when you are out walking, especially if you are in a quiet place in nature.

~ Decide where you are going to send the illumined grace. What archangel qualities does this person, place or situation need?

~ Create a vast cosmic archangel gem in your mind's eye and ask a unicorn to illumine it.

~ Visualize the cosmic gem moving through space and time to the person, place or situation that needs to be healed, strengthened, purified or brought peace.

~ See it resting there, radiating and pulsing intense and glorious combined archangel and unicorn light.

~ Know that it is raising the frequency of that person, place or situation.

Unicorns, Archangel Michael and Sapphires

The Sapphire Ray is a combination of the Blue Ray of Healing and Communication, the Yellow of Knowledge and Wisdom and the Red of Action. This is a potent mixture of power and integrity.

Archangel Michael, the sapphire-blue archangel, offers you protection, courage, strength, honour, truth and trust, among other qualities. He is in charge of the development of the throat chakras of individuals and humanity in general, as well as the throat chakra of the planet. Sapphires are the physicalized form of his energy, and when used correctly, they connect you to him. They help you act with total integrity, in alignment with your God-self.

EXPERIENCING ARCHANGEL MICHAEL'S ETHERIC NINTH-DIMENSIONAL COSMIC SAPPHIRE ILLUMINATED BY UNICORNS

~ Find a place where you can be quiet and undisturbed.

~ Light a candle if possible to raise the energy and focus your intention.

~ Close your eyes and breathe comfortably until you feel relaxed.

~ Archangel Michael, in his deep-blue robe, is standing in front of you.

~ He is holding a beautiful deep-blue sapphire, which is sparkling and twinkling with light.

~ Mentally say, 'Beloved Archangel Michael, I ask you to create an ethereal ninth-dimensional cosmic sapphire for me.'

~ See or sense him smile in agreement.

~ As he holds the sapphire in front of you, watch it slowly expand, becoming lighter in colour as it does so.

~ As it becomes paler and more translucent, it shimmers with light and power.

~ Archangel Michael mentally asks you to prepare yourself to receive it.

~ Relax and be receptive.

~ Very slowly, he raises the vast cosmic sapphire, holding courage, strength, truth, integrity, honesty, power and his light, over your head.

~ He brings it slowly down over you until you are sitting or standing in the centre of this vast etheric gem.

~ Take a few moments to experience this.

~ Then mentally call a unicorn and ask it to enter and activate the cosmic sapphire.

~ Be aware of a pure white unicorn touching the cosmic gem with its horn of light.

~ The unicorn light fills the cosmic sapphire and flows in wave after wave through you.

~ Absorb it in deep silence.

~ Magic and miracles can now take place.

~ You can open your eyes and return to waking reality or continue by sending out the cosmic sapphire with unicorn energy to help the world (as follows).

WORKING WITH THE COSMIC SAPPHIRE WITH UNICORN ENERGY

~ Float to the White House in Washington, DC, and place the cosmic sapphire over it. Then do the same with the European Parliament in Brussels, Belgium, the Houses of Parliament in the UK and any other places where decisions are made.

~ Ask unicorns and Archangel Michael to ensure that decisions in these places are made with integrity and that there is higher communication with honesty.

~ Send the cosmic sapphire to individuals and groups that need the courage to stand up for themselves or their beliefs.

~ Use it in any way that is for your highest good and that of the planet.

~ Thank the archangel and the unicorns.

Unicorns, Archangel Raphael and Emeralds

The Emerald Ray is a combination of the Blue Ray of Healing with the Yellow Ray of Knowledge and Wisdom. It lights up the third eye and stimulates the heart chakra.

Archangel Raphael, the emerald green archangel, is the angel of healing and abundance. In charge of the development of the third eye chakra of individuals and humanity, he opens you up to enlightenment, to seeing the whole of life from a spiritual perspective. He also shows you how to attain abundance consciousness. When you have full abundance consciousness, you totally understand that you are 100 per cent responsible for creating your destiny. Therefore you can draw from the generous and benevolent universe whatever you believe you deserve.

Archangel Raphael also heals under grace. Emeralds are the materialized form of his energy. They bring clarity of mind, loyalty, friendship, trust, healing, prosperity and other qualities.

EXPERIENCING ARCHANGEL RAPHAEL'S ETHERIC NINTH-DIMENSIONAL COSMIC EMERALD ILLUMINATED BY UNICORNS

~ Let yourself sink into relaxation once more.

~ Archangel Raphael, shimmering with emerald light, is approaching you.

~ He is holding a vibrant, sparkling deep-green emerald and smiles into your eyes as he holds it out to you.

~ Mentally say, 'Beloved Archangel Raphael, I ask you to create an ethereal ninth-dimensional cosmic emerald for me.'

~ See or sense him nod in agreement.

~ As he holds the emerald in front of you, watch it slowly expand, becoming lighter in colour as it does so.

~ As it becomes paler and more translucent, it shimmers with light and truth.

~ Archangel Raphael mentally asks you to prepare yourself to receive it.

~ Relax and be receptive.

~ Very slowly, he raises the vast cosmic emerald, holding healing energy, clarity of mind, loyalty, friendship, abundance consciousness, higher enlightenment, trust and his light, over your head.

~ He brings it slowly down over you until you are sitting or standing in the centre of this vast etheric gem.

~ Take a few moments to experience this.

~ Then mentally call a unicorn and ask it to enter and activate the cosmic emerald.

~ Be aware of a pure white unicorn touching the cosmic gem with its horn of light.

~ The unicorn light fills the cosmic emerald and engulfs you.

~ Absorb it in silence, allowing deep transformation to take place.

~ You can open your eyes and return to waking reality or continue by sending out the cosmic emerald illuminated with unicorn energy to help the world.

WORKING WITH THE COSMIC EMERALD WITH UNICORN ENERGY

~ Float the cosmic emerald to hospitals and healing temples. Bring it down over the buildings and hold them in higher healing energy.

~ Send it to someone to hold them in their perfect health blueprint.

~ Let it float to Table Mountain, the great portal for abundance in South Africa, to open it up so that it can spread abundance consciousness to the world.

~ Thank the archangel and the unicorns.

Unicorns, Archangel Uriel and Rubies

The Ruby Ray is a combination of red for action, gold for wisdom and blue for peace and higher communication.

Archangel Uriel, the ruby-red and gold archangel, is the angel of peace and wisdom. He encourages those who are ready for intergalactic responsibility to become galactic masters.

He is in charge of the development of the solar plexus chakras of humanity and the planet. Rubies contain his concentrated energy. They bring confidence, self-worth, wisdom and the ability to take action.

EXPERIENCING ARCHANGEL URIEL'S ETHERIC NINTH-DIMENSIONAL COSMIC RUBY ILLUMINATED BY UNICORNS

~ Let yourself sink into relaxation.

~ Archangel Uriel, shimmering with ruby light, is approaching you.

~ He is holding a glowing deep-red ruby, which he holds out to you as a gift.

~ Lovingly reach out a hand to touch it.

~ Then mentally say, 'Beloved Archangel Uriel, I ask you to create an ethereal ninth-dimensional cosmic ruby for me.'

~ See or sense him nod in agreement.

~ As he holds the ruby in front of you, watch it slowly expand, becoming lighter in colour as it does so.

~ As it becomes paler and more translucent, it shimmers with light and faith.

~ Archangel Uriel asks you to prepare yourself to receive it.

~ Relax and be receptive.

~ Very slowly, he raises the vast cosmic ruby, filled with the energy of peace, higher communication, confidence, self-worth, wisdom, power and his light, over your head.

~ He brings it slowly down over you until you are sitting or standing in the centre of this vast etheric gem.

~ Take a few moments to experience this.

~ Then mentally call a unicorn and ask it to enter and activate the cosmic ruby.

~ Be aware of a pure white unicorn touching the cosmic gem with its horn of light.

~ The unicorn light fills the cosmic ruby and flows through you.

~ Absorb it in silence, allowing deep transformation to take place.

~ You can open your eyes and return to waking reality or continue by sending out the cosmic ruby illuminated with unicorn energy to help the world.

Working with the Cosmic Ruby with Unicorn Energy

~ Send the cosmic ruby illuminated with unicorn energy to parts of the world where people are downtrodden.

~ Bring it down over schools or other places where children need confidence and self-worth.

~ Ask unicorns to place it in parts of the world where there is conflict, in order to radiate peace.

~ Thank the archangel and the unicorns.

Unicorns, Archangel Gabriel and Diamonds

The glittering Diamond-White Ray carries the qualities of all the colour rays.

Archangel Gabriel, the shimmering white archangel, is overseeing the purification of the entire world. He is in charge of the base, sacral and navel chakras of individuals and the planet. Through the base chakra, he helps people find balance and self-discipline; through the sacral chakra, he helps them heal and develop transcendent love; and through the navel, he brings a universal understanding of oneness. The diamond is the physical form of his light and shimmers with purity, joy, clarity and everlasting promise.

EXPERIENCING ARCHANGEL GABRIEL'S ETHERIC NINTH-DIMENSIONAL COSMIC DIAMOND ILLUMINATED BY UNICORNS

~ Breathe comfortably until you feel really relaxed.

~ Archangel Gabriel, shimmering with pure white light, is approaching you.

~ He is holding a wonderful sparkling diamond, which he offers to you.

~ Lovingly reach out a hand to touch it.

~ Then mentally say, 'Beloved Archangel Gabriel, I ask you to create an ethereal ninth-dimensional cosmic diamond for me.'

~ See or sense him nod in agreement.

~ As he holds the diamond in front of you, watch it slowly expand, becoming lighter in colour as it does so.

~ As it becomes more translucent, it shimmers with rainbow light.

~ Archangel Gabriel asks you to prepare yourself to receive it.

~ Relax and be receptive.

~ Very slowly, he raises the vast cosmic diamond, filled with the energy of clarity, purity, joy, oneness, unconditional love, the ability to take wise decisions and his archangel light, over your head.

~ He brings it slowly down over you until you are sitting or standing in the centre of this vast etheric gem.

~ Take a few moments to experience this.

~ Then mentally call a unicorn and ask it to enter and activate the cosmic diamond.

~ Be aware of a pure white unicorn touching the cosmic gem with its horn of light.

~ The unicorn light fills the cosmic diamond and flows through you.

~ Absorb it in silence, allowing deep transformation to take place.

~ You can open your eyes and return to waking reality or continue by sending out the cosmic diamond illuminated with unicorn energy to help the world.

WORKING WITH THE COSMIC DIAMOND WITH UNICORN ENERGY

~ Send the cosmic diamond illuminated with unicorn energy to parts of the world where people are bewildered and seek clarity.

~ Bring it down over refugee camps, prisons, schools or other places where people need joy.

~ Ask unicorns to position it over places where choices are made, so that the decision-makers have inspiration and wisdom.

~ Thank the archangel and the unicorns.

Unicorns, Archangel Christiel and Pearls

The luminous, iridescent Pearl Ray is one of the new ninth-dimensional rays beaming down to Earth. It carries higher love, purity, peace, courage and Christ Light.

Archangel Christiel, the archangel of peace, oversees the Stargate of Lyra, the unicorns' entry point into this universe. The pearl is the physical form of his light. It glows with the Divine Feminine qualities of love, caring, nurturing, beauty, creativity, peace, enlightenment and inner happiness.

Archangel Christiel is in charge of our causal chakra and that of the planet. Archangel Joules, the angel in charge of the oceans, also adds his light to a natural pearl, as it develops around a piece of grit or some foreign body in an oyster in the oceans.

EXPERIENCING ARCHANGEL CHRISTIEL'S ETHERIC NINTH-DIMENSIONAL COSMIC PEARL ILLUMINATED BY ARCHANGEL JOULES AND UNICORNS

~ If possible, drink a glass of water before this connection, for the cosmic pearl is of the element of water.

~ Allow yourself to sink into a comfortable relaxed state and close your eyes.

~ Imagine yourself sitting by a peaceful ocean on a moonlit night.

~ Archangel Christiel, in his shimmering silver-white light, is standing in front of you.

~ He is holding a magnificent pearl, which is glowing with light.

~ Mentally say, 'Beloved Archangel Christiel, I ask you to create an ethereal ninth-dimensional cosmic pearl for me.'

~ See or sense him smile in agreement.

~ Watch the pearl slowly expand, becoming lighter in colour as it does so.

~ As it becomes transparent and more translucent, it shimmers with light and peace.

~ Archangel Christiel mentally asks you to prepare yourself to receive it.

~ Relax and open yourself up.

~ Very slowly, he raises the vast cosmic pearl, holding peace, Divine Feminine wisdom and his light, over your head.

~ He brings it slowly down over you until you are sitting or standing in the centre of this vast etheric gem.

~ Then Archangel Joules, angel of the oceans, enters in his blue-green robes and touches the cosmic pearl with love. Feel this.

~ Now mentally call a unicorn and ask it to enter and activate the cosmic pearl.

~ See or sense a pure white unicorn touching the cosmic gem with its horn of light.

~ The unicorn light fills the cosmic pearl and flows through you.

~ Absorb it in deep silence.

~ You can open your eyes and return to waking reality or continue by sending out the cosmic pearl illuminated with unicorn energy to help the world.

WORKING WITH THE COSMIC PEARL
WITH UNICORN ENERGY

~ Send the cosmic pearl illuminated with unicorn energy to parts of the world that are still masculine dominated and need the influence of the Divine Feminine.

~ Let it float into the oceans to light up and purify the waters.

~ Let it rest above the world, sending its light to women everywhere and touching them with Divine Feminine wisdom.

~ Thank the archangel and the unicorns.

CHAPTER 27

Unicorns and Crystals

O ne of the factors that enabled the Atlanteans to create the fabled Golden Age with its extraordinary spiritual technology was their understanding of crystals. The High Priests and Priestesses of that time taught that crystals had a consciousness and an energy that could be harnessed and used. The Atlanteans activated crystals to light their homes, power their vehicles and provide all the energy that they needed. Many crystal adepts of that time have reincarnated now to bring their special knowledge back to the planet.

Unicorn Crystals

Selenite

The highly evolved people of Atlantis worked with unicorns and recognized that the crystal selenite had a particular resonance with them. I love selenite's milky white softness and have pieces of it all over my home. I place tiny strips on the lintels above the doors and on cupboards, so that unicorn energy streams in and bathes people who walk past.

Selenite does not need to be cleansed, for it has an inner radiance. It dissolves in water, so don't leave it out in the rain or soaking in the bath for very long.

Quartz

Unicorns also love to connect with us through quartz crystals, which have a pure, clear energy and can be easily programmed.

If you work with quartz, you may need to cleanse it. There are many ways to do this. You can play a singing bowl over it, chant the sacred 'Om', wash it in water, put it in uncooked rice or blow on it. You can also charge it with sound or by leaving it by a waterfall or out in the moonlight, especially at Full Moon.

Using a Unicorn Crystal

When you use your unicorn crystal, it is automatically charged with Christ Light, so it pulls lower energy out of a person, situation or place and replaces it with unconditional love.

Here is an example. I know someone who lived in a cul-de-sac where several marriages were breaking up and some violence had occurred. She charged a crystal with unicorn energy and placed it on a street map of her area, on her road. Not only did the separations stop, but some of the couples got back together again.

Setting Your Intention

Whichever crystal you choose to use, it is worth spending some time deciding what you really, truly want the unicorn energy to do. Whether it is a personal vision or something for humanity or the planet, your focused intent is powerful. If you were playing darts and wanted to aim for the bullseye, for example, it would be ridiculous to envision your missile going into the two or six. You would think about the bullseye.

Once you have decided what you want your crystal and unicorn energy to do, you may like to hold your crystal to your third eye and dedicate it to your work. It is even more powerful if you put it to your throat and say, whisper or think what you want it to accomplish. Then put it to your third eye for a moment.

Here are some suggestions: 'I dedicate this crystal to connecting me with my unicorn,' or 'I intend this crystal to use unicorn energy to bring me more like-minded friends.'

As long as your focus is for the highest good of all, you can place any wish into your crystal.

Setting Your Intention under the Law of Grace

If you are not certain if your wish is for the highest good, set it under the Law of Grace. For example, if you wish to send healing to a person or animal, send it under grace, as healing will contravene the dictates of their soul if they need to learn from the illness. Grace means that you have released any personal desire for that person or animal to be better. You have simply sent the energy and let it go. That way, your ego is not involved and therefore no karma can be incurred.

Another example would be if you wanted to buy a particular house or be offered a specific job. Again, you should set your intention under grace, for there may be a higher plan.

Naturally, unicorns would never do anything that contravened the demands of anyone's Higher Self. However, once their energy has been connected to a crystal, it is very powerful and magic can happen. Using the Law of Grace is a way of protecting yourself from any karmic consequences.

Once you have set your intention, your unicorn crystal will be working energetically to bring about your vision. You can carry it with you or place it somewhere special. You may wish to set up a unicorn crystal altar.

Setting Up a Unicorn Crystal Altar

An altar is a sacred place devoted to spirit. It radiates a high and powerful vibration if its intention and purity are maintained.

Size is not important. Even a small altar, such as part of a shelf or a small table, can emit a very strong high-frequency light. Nor does the altar have to be on display. If you wish to create an altar in your bedroom or your office, you can place it in a drawer, where it is not immediately visible but is just as effective.

MAKING A UNICORN CRYSTAL ALTAR

~ First find a place, however small, that you can use solely for your altar. It can be indoors or outside. If it is indoors, you may like to place a special cloth on it, perhaps a golden one or white one. If this is not possible, use what you have, for intention is more powerful than physical perfection! If it is outside, nature may provide a mossy corner or a flat stone or a section of a flowerbed for you.

~ Whether your altar is indoors or outdoors, if children, dogs, foxes or people mess it up, stay calm, centred and in harmony! Decide that you can now create something even better and set about doing so, possibly in a different location.

~ Many objects are suitable for your unicorn crystal altar. If possible, try to find something to represent each of the four elements – fire, earth, air and water. You may like to add a candle for fire, for example. Or you can cut out a picture of a fire, find a little model fire dragon or add a piece of red cloth. You can use a pebble (a white one if possible) or a crystal or some earth to symbolize the element of earth. A feather is often used for air, but you may prefer a dandelion seed or a picture of a bird. A bowl of water or vase of flowers with water in it can symbolize water.

~ Bless any item that you love, such as a shell, photo, picture of an ascended master or deck of unicorn cards, and place it on your unicorn altar.

~ And remember to place a charged unicorn crystal there. Its power will be multiplied.

CHAPTER 28

Unicorn Crystal Grids

A crystal grid is a powerful symbol that activates cosmic energies and can create great change. It can be simple or complex and be made up of crystals or white pebbles, large or small. The most important thing is the intention you place into it.

Unicorn crystal grids are tremendously effective. I once had a Violet Flame unicorn crystal grid made up of amethyst, selenite and white pebbles laid out on a small table in my conservatory. The intention was that it would transmute any negative energy in my home. One day a friend came for coffee and we were chatting about all sorts of things. Suddenly she asked, 'Why has that grid suddenly lit up?' I explained its purpose and we realized that we had been talking about something rather dire that had been on the news. True to its purpose, the Violet Flame and unicorn grid had transmuted the negativity. Someone who had a similar grid told me that it lit up whenever the news was on.

Don't underestimate the power of a grid. Once when I was working on a business project with a colleague, I laid out a unicorn crystal grid to hold everything together and indeed the project went very well. Then one day I looked at the grid and decided it looked a bit tired and dusty, so I dismantled it. The very next morning I had a new awareness about my colleague. I saw some things in a very different light and the entire project collapsed. That grid had accomplished its task and held everything together, and I presume that when it was no longer suitable for that to happen, the unicorns subtly nudged me and encouraged me to release it.

Setting Up a Unicorn Crystal Grid

First decide what you want your unicorn crystal grid to accomplish. Here are some examples of the work that they can do:

- Hold your home in peace and harmony.

- Hold the energy of something you want to happen.

- Keep your chakras fifth-dimensional.

- Bring the perfect job, project or home forward for you.

- Help you to manifest the desires of your soul.

CREATING AND ACTIVATING A UNICORN CRYSTAL GRID TO MANIFEST THE DESIRES OF YOUR SOUL

~ Decide what you wish to manifest. Make sure it is something that gives you joy and soul satisfaction.

~ Write it down. This makes it clear and adds energy to it.

~ Decide what shape your grid should be. The shape that you choose triggers the cosmic energies needed to fulfil your intention. Simple circles, squares and triangles are very effective.

Eleven is a very sacred number. It indicates bringing something in at a higher level than before and attracts energies to fulfil soul desires. So here are the steps you can take to create and activate this grid with the vibration of 11:

~ Choose 11 selenite or clear quartz crystals, or white pebbles. Wash any quartz crystals or pebbles and bless them all. I like to hold the stones, pebbles or crystals in my hands and ask unicorns to bless them.

~ Place a special pebble or crystal, then place the others round it in a circle, a square or whatever shape you have chosen. Create whatever geometric shape feels right.

~ If you have selenite strips or Lemurian or quartz wands, radiate them out from your grid.

~ Be as creative as you wish with your grid. White flowers and a white candle vibrate beautifully with the purity of unicorns, so they will enhance the energy.

~ Close your eyes as you invoke unicorns.

~ Then touch each stone or crystal with a crystal wand or with your finger.

~ Take the stone from the centre and hold it lightly in your cupped hands.

~ Breathe white light slowly into your body, and on each out-breath, let white light fill your aura.

~ Know that the white light is entering the grid and activating the manifestation of your soul desires.

A Unicorn Cosmic Diamond Violet Flame Crystal Grid

The Violet Flame, which is in the charge of Archangel Zadkiel and St Germain, the Lord of Civilization, is a very powerful tool for transmutation. It was used by everyone during the Golden Era of Atlantis to help keep the energy pure and clear, for it consumes and transforms all lower frequencies. When the light of Atlantis diminished, the Violet Flame was withdrawn from general use because the people could no longer be trusted to use it for the highest good. At the Harmonic Convergence in 1987, so many people world-wide prayed for assistance for humanity that St Germain petitioned Source for its return.

Within a few years the Violet Flame merged with the Silver Flame of Grace and Harmony and then the Gold Ray to form the Gold and Silver Violet Flame. In 2015, as an awesome gift to assist the ascension of humanity, Archangels Gabriel and Zadkiel merged their energy to create the Cosmic Diamond Violet Flame, which is a very pure high-frequency energy. Archangel Gabriel's diamond shreds and dissipates anything that no longer serves the greater good. Unicorns vibrate perfectly with the pure white Archangel Gabriel.

Archangel Zadkiel's energy is encapsulated in amethyst crystals, so if you can find some amethyst for this grid to anchor the Violet Flame, that would be excellent. However, it is not essential.

The Violet Flame opens up our energy centres, so I always call in the Gold Ray of Christ as a shield whenever I invoke it. If you have a piece of citrine or a little citrine tumblestone, which holds Christ Light, it will add protection to your grid.

The symbol for this grid is a six-pointed star, with the amethyst in the centre. To lay out a six-pointed star I find it easy and effective to create an 'X' and then make a vertical line down through it with selenite strips. I like to add a citrine tumblestone to draw in the Gold Ray of Christ and a Herkimer diamond for Archangel Gabriel. But even if it is simply made with pebbles from your garden, the power of your focused intention will make this unicorn crystal grid very effective.

CREATING AND ACTIVATING A COSMIC DIAMOND VIOLET FLAME GRID

~ Decide on your intention. Here are some possibilities:

  – To transmute any lower vibrations round you and then raise your frequency so that unicorns can hold you in the fifth dimension.

  – To hold the Cosmic Diamond Violet Flame in your home, your office or a specific area on the planet to clear lower energies and hold that place at a higher frequency.

  – To bathe a situation or person in the Cosmic Diamond Violet Flame.

~ Focus on your intention as you build the grid and bless the crystals or pebbles as you place them. Remember that flowers, candles, suitable photographs and holy statues all add light to your grid.

~ Invoke Archangels Zadkiel and Gabriel, Christ Light and unicorns and ask them to work with your grid.

~ Activate the grid by touching each stone or crystal in turn, mentally blessing and thanking them. You can do this with a crystal wand, a Lemurian crystal or your finger.

~ Let your Cosmic Diamond Violet Flame grid do its work.

~ Recharge it each day or when you feel it needs a boost, by touching the stones with intention.

Making a Unicorn Crystal Grid for Blessing and Healing

This unicorn grid brings you unicorn blessings and healing. You can also set it to radiate blessings and healing to others.

Unicorns bless you with the qualities you need
in order to accomplish your soul mission.

Until 2015 only seventh-dimensional unicorns were able to help humanity. Now ninth and 10th-dimensional ones can help you by connecting to this crystal grid.

ACTIVATING AND WORKING WITH A UNICORN CRYSTAL GRID FOR BLESSING AND HEALING

SET YOUR INTENTION

~ Your intention may be to heal and bless yourself, or to offer healing and blessings to someone else, or a group of people, or a situation or place. You may want to heal karmic or ancestral wounds or to bless your own or someone else's divine mission. You can even ask to bring enlightenment to yourself, a politician, a school administrator or any group that makes decisions.

~ When you have decided on the purpose of your grid, light a candle.

~   Again, you can create any shape you wish. I like to make this particular grid in the form of a long triangle to reflect the outline of the unicorn horn. Then I radiate selenite strips from it to allow the wish or intention to be sent out.

CREATE A CEREMONY TO EMPOWER YOUR INTENTION

Ceremonies are very powerful and you may wish to create one to enhance the potency of your intention. Several people working together will enhance the activation of this crystal grid and ritual or ceremony will add energy to it.

Make sure you are working in a cleansed, high-frequency space. To achieve this you may like to:

~   Call in the Cosmic Diamond Violet Flame to transmute any lower energies and light up the area.

~   Ask fire dragons to burn up any lower energies and place an etheric firewall round the grid.

~   Cleanse the space with incense sticks, clapping or angel spray.

~   Use crystal bowls, humming, chanting or music to raise the frequency.

~   Light candles or add flowers.

~   Add anything ceremonial that feels right to you.

INVOKE UNICORNS

As you know, a unicorn will come to you if you send out a thought inviting it. However, for this grid, you may wish to make a special invocation with intent, as follows.

~   Invoke unicorns three times, either mentally or aloud, with the words: 'I now invoke unicorns, unicorns, unicorns.'

~ Pause and then say this prayer: 'Please connect your energy to me and link me to the grid so that I may use the healing and blessings you activate for the greatest good of all. So be it. It is done.'

ACTIVATE AND ENERGIZE THE GRID

~ Hold your hands over the grid to energize it.

~ Touch each stone or crystal with a crystal wand.

~ Remember to thank the unicorns.

You may also like to use the following visualization.

ENERGIZING A UNICORN CRYSTAL GRID FOR BLESSING AND HEALING

~ Sit near your unicorn crystal grid, holding a crystal wand, and close your eyes.

~ Imagine the radiance of a Full Moon bathing your inner scene with magical milky-white light.

~ Call in unicorns and quietly wait as one floats along a moonbeam towards you.

~ Feel its love, peace, serenity and joy.

~ It is pouring showers of blessings from its horn over you. Relax and let them fill your energy fields. Know that something is being awakened in you.

~ Take all the time you need to explain your request for healing and blessing and who it is for.

~ When you have finished, the great pure white unicorn bends its head so that its horn touches the crystal wand you are holding, filling it with the blessings and healing energy you have asked for.

~ Now a shaft of pure white light appears beside you.

~ Your unicorn invites you to ride on its back and kneels down so that you can climb easily onto it.

~ You and the unicorn are moving lightly, happily and safely straight up the shaft through the dimensions until you see the steps leading up to the Light of Source.

~ Glorious Seraphim greet you and sing over you. You hand one of them your crystal wand and it takes it into the hallowed presence.

~ At last it reappears and you see your crystal wand is awake and beaming with light.

~ The Seraphim hands it to you, its eyes bathing you in purest love.

~ The unicorn brings you back down the shaft to the place you started from.

~ Thank it for coming to you and taking you on this journey.

~ Open your eyes and be very aware of the crystal wand in your hand.

~ When you are ready, place it in the crystal grid.

~ Relax over the next days and weeks, allowing the unicorns and the crystal grid to work with the universal energies for the highest good of all.

PART IV

UNICORNS AND CHAKRAS

CHAPTER 29

Unicorns Light Up
Your 12 Chakras

In the Golden Era of Atlantis everyone had 12 fully operational chakras that vibrated at the higher levels of the fifth dimension. This enabled them to live in love, peace and harmony. It also allowed them all to enjoy advanced psychic gifts and develop the awesome powers of spiritual technology.

In the 10,000 years since the fall of Atlantis, we have been living in a third-dimensional world and have only had seven small lower-frequency chakras active. Now that we are seriously preparing for the new Golden Age, many of us are living in a more spiritual way and are anchoring our 12 fifth-dimensional chakras. By 2032, almost everyone must have them all open and activated.

During the 1,500-year Golden Era of Atlantis, all the people were aware of the shimmering white spiritual unicorns around them. These beings of light poured blessings over all the citizens to help them maintain their purity. Everyone knew their own personal unicorn, who helped their chakras remain clear and open. This was one of the important factors in holding the vibration of the golden years.

As we move towards the new Golden Age of Aquarius starting in 2032, unicorns are connecting with individuals who are bringing their spiritual centres into alignment with the higher frequencies now flowing into the planet. Recently, they agreed to work with our chakras. Soon after 2032, they will have connected with most people to light them up on their ascension paths.

Unicorns assist in the establishment of
the 12 fifth-dimensional chakras.

How Unicorns Help Your Chakras to Develop

Unicorns naturally co-operate with archangels, who hold the blueprint, the potential and highest possibilities for each of your chakras. Archangels support, activate and light each centre up, while unicorns direct energy from their horns into each one to energize and illuminate it. They work particularly with the third eye and the heart, but they can boost all the chakras. They also shower light into your energy fields, which accelerates the transformation of your chakras. They help your chakras to develop in several ways:

Expansion

When a unicorn sends its power into one of your chakras, it doesn't simply illuminate it, it expands it. A 30centimetre (6inch) diameter chakra may become a 60centimetre (1foot) diameter one, for example. In illumined souls, chakras may even become a kilometre wide, with fingers of energy reaching out into the cosmos. Your spiritual energy centres are unlimited in scope!

Purification

Each chakra has a certain number of petals or chambers containing lessons and experiences that you have to undertake and master before that chakra can fully open. When unicorns pour their pure, shimmering white energy into your chakras, as long as the chamber doors are open, it can enter the chambers and purify anything within them that needs to be cleansed.

Balance

Even in the golden years of Atlantis, chakras could become unbalanced, and this was the cause of any dis-ease or ill health. At that time the priesthood was able to bring the chakras back into balance for perfect health, and unicorns (and temple cats) would often help with this. Even now, if you are only slightly off-centre, your unicorn can realign your chakras.

The Ignition of Higher Possibilities

Within your energy centres are held the keys and codes of higher possibilities. Most humans do not fully realize the potential encoded within them or who they truly are, and it may take a boost of unicorn energy for their true light to emerge.

The Maintenance of a High Frequency

If you are in a place or among people where the energy is low, it can be challenging to sustain a high vibration. If you are in such a situation, call in unicorns, for they can add their pearlescent light to all your energy centres, so that they maintain a high frequency no matter what your surroundings.

If the lower emotion comes from within you, as a result of loss or disappointment for example, ask unicorns to hold you steady.

Bringing Forward Wisdom

You almost certainly have access to more inner wisdom than you realize. Sometimes people are so set in their patterns or ideas of self-worth that they don't plumb the depths of their own knowing. But the unicorns' Divine Feminine light allows you to activate and bring forward the wisdom held within your chakras.

The Development of Psychic Abilities

We are all psychic, but most people distrust their instincts and intuition. The greatest source of psychic connection is your heart centre. When you work with unicorns, they enable you to bring forward the knowing and wisdom of your heart.

The Lighting Up of the 12 Chakras

Unicorns will send a shaft of high-frequency light through your 12 chakras, illuminating them all gloriously.

The Cosmic Chakras

Planets and stars are the chakras of the universe. Some, like Orion, are fully ascended. Others, like Sirius, have an ascended aspect only. As already mentioned, the ascended part of Sirius is called Lakumay.

You may well have already connected your personal chakras to the cosmic ones. If you are engaged with this chapter, you are ready for the next step, which is allowing unicorns to make it a two-way connection.

> *Unicorns make a two-way connection from*
> *your personal chakras to the cosmic ones and*
> *activate the cosmic codes within you.*

Making a Two-Way Connection with the Cosmic Chakras

Unicorns can light up the codes in your personal chakras so that they can reach out and connect to their cosmic counterparts. Unicorn energy can then strengthen the return connection from that star to you, so that you can download stellar information and wisdom.

For example, unicorn energy can light up the codes in your Earth Star chakra to enable it to link to Neptune and its ascended part, Toutillay. Then they can support the energy flowing down from Toutillay to your Earth Star and ignite the higher codes there. I will expand on this in the following chapters.

I have shared elsewhere about the time I was walking in a meditative way in the woods and spontaneously my 12 chakras all opened. Suddenly beams of light radiated out from each one to the relevant stars and my energy fields became enormous. Unicorns formed this energy into a vast cosmic Orb and at that awesome moment I realized we are all stars in our own right and connected to everything.

Now unicorns are energizing the return of knowledge and wisdom from the stars and planets, as they did in the Golden Era of Atlantis.

CHAPTER 30

Unicorns and
the Earth Star Chakra

Archangel Sandalphon is in charge of the development of
your Earth Star chakra. He is known as one of the tall
angels, because his energy reaches from the centre of Earth right
up to the Godhead. His twin flame, Archangel Metatron, is the
other tall angel.

Your Earth Star is below your feet. It is and always has been
fifth-dimensional. It was withdrawn at the fall of Atlantis, when
the planet could no longer sustain the higher frequency. Now it
has been returned to us. When you make it magnificent through
spiritual practice and pure intention, Archangel Sandalphon
switches its light on and it becomes incredibly powerful.

Your Earth Star chakra is your grounding chakra for
ascension. When you are third-dimensional with no divine
aspirations, you are inhabiting a spiritual bungalow, so your
base chakra is sufficient foundation for you. However, when
you connect with angels and unicorns and start to ascend, you
aim to construct a spiritual skyscraper or castle. Then you need

a much bigger, deeper, more solid foundation, reaching right into the heart of Lady Gaia. Your Earth Star chakra is that fifth-dimensional foundation, a most beautiful place where the blueprint for your incarnation and your divine potential is held.

*If you invite a unicorn to bless and light up
your Earth Star, you create a paradise.*

As your Earth Star chakra rises in frequency, it changes colour. It starts as black and white, then becomes dark grey, then lighter grey and finally, when it is fully awake, shimmering, sparkling silver.

Your Earth Star is also about your relationship with the Earth and with Lady Gaia. It contains 33 chambers, each of which holds a lesson for you to learn. You may already have mastered some or all of these in other lives, in which case those particular chambers will be open and lit up.

Unicorns can make the lights that are already on in the chambers shine even more brightly. This enables you to see more of your divine blueprint and therefore your potential, gifts and talents. If you regularly work with your Earth Star chakra and ask unicorns to activate the keys and codes of your divine potential, it will advance your ascension journey considerably.

Your Unified Column of Light

When all 12 of your fifth-dimensional chakras are established, balanced, energized and activated, they form a unified column of light. Unicorns flood their pure energy through this integrated column of light and this flows down into your shimmering silver

Earth Star, which then expands hugely and lights up with a pearlescent glow.

Hollow Earth

When the energy from your unified column of light floods into your Earth Star chakra, it pours down through golden roots into Serapis Bey's Golden Crystal Pyramid in Hollow Earth. Here this mighty master gathers the Earth Star energy of everyone in the world and passes it to three mighty angelic beings to light up the ley lines of the planet and the cosmos. These are Lady Gaia, who is a Throne and is the ninth-dimensional angel who ensouls Earth; Roquiel, who is of the Seraphim vibration; and Archangel Gersisa. They work in the centre of the Earth. We tend to think of the centre of our planet as rock or gas. In fact, the Hollow Earth chakra is an inconceivably vast and light seventh-dimensional paradise with its own Sun.

Connecting to the Cosmic Earth Star

When the light from your personal Earth Star chakra is bright enough, your unicorn facilitates a pure connection from it to Neptune and its ascended part, Toutillay. Here the higher knowledge, information and secrets of Atlantis and Lemuria are held within a sacred Orb.

The next step is for the unicorn energy to access and light a flame within the sacred Orb of Toutillay. Then magic happens and the divine wisdom of Atlantis and Lemuria pour down the shaft of unicorn light into your Earth Star chakra. You then help the planet and many people onto their ascension paths. You become an instrument to return the Great Light of Atlantis and Lemuria to the Earth.

Here's a visualization to help you make the connection:

CONNECTING YOUR EARTH STAR TO NEPTUNE

~ Find a place where you can be quiet and undisturbed.

~ Close your eyes and breathe yourself into your inner world.

~ Focus on your Earth Star chakra below your feet and see it as a huge ball. What colour is it?

~ Archangel Sandalphon is holding it steady.

~ You are now in the centre of the chakra and can see the treasure chest containing your divine blueprint and potential. How big is it? Is it open or closed?

~ You can see 33 chambers spiralling out from the centre of the chakra. How many doors are open? How many are closed?

~ Invoke your unicorn and immediately it is standing in front of you, illuminating your Earth Star chakra with white light.

~ Then it is taking you to Neptune, where the mighty masters of Neptune, the 12 great cosmic beings who look after the planet, greet you warmly.

~ They point to a great door, which opens up to Inner Neptune, the ascended part, Toutillay.

~ You enter a chamber filled with the secret and sacred knowledge of Atlantis and Lemuria. It is available to you. Absorb what you are ready to accept.

~ Your unicorn now radiates a shaft of white light through the cosmos to your Earth Star chakra.

~   Keys and codes of the ancient wisdom pour down the shaft into your treasure chest, which opens wide. How big is it now?

~   Chambers that were previously closed are opening.

~   Take your divine blueprint out of your treasure chest and see it illuminated.

~   Sense your entire Earth Star chakra expand as light pours down through it into the Golden Crystal Pyramid of Hollow Earth.

~   Serapis Bey collects the light and passes it to Lady Gaia, the Seraphim Roquiel and Archangel Gersisa.

~   They accept the light and spread it round the ley lines.

~   The entire planet is lighting up and pulsing with new energy.

~   Relax for a moment before you open your eyes.

CHAPTER 31

Unicorns and
the Base Chakra

The base chakras of humanity, at the base of the spine, have undergone a dramatic change in recent years as they have been transforming from third-dimensional red to the magnificent platinum light of the fifth dimension. The base centre has been the root for thousands of years, during which people relied very much on the family and local community to be their source of security. The changing world has uprooted much of this, forcing individuals to create a deeper spiritual foundation. Trusting the spiritual world is a step towards both enlightenment and ascension.

The base chakra is overseen by Archangel Gabriel, the pure white archangel of purity, joy and clarity. Being pure white, he has a natural affinity with unicorns. When they add their light to his energy, it becomes a translucent diamond, vibrating at an even higher frequency. This enables the chakras developed by Archangel Gabriel to move more quickly into higher ascension.

As your fifth-dimensional energy becomes stronger, your base centre radiates more platinum light. When this happens, you feel happy, harmonious and safe, and it helps you to understand your true magnificence.

The base chakra is known as the seat of the soul, for when it holds platinum light, you can start to merge with your Higher Self to achieve spiritual enlightenment. When unicorns add their ineffable light to this chakra, your kundalini flows faster and more gloriously and helps to build your Antakarana bridge, the rainbow bridge to your Monad and ultimately to Source.

The Chambers of the Base Chakra

There are only two chambers in the base chakra. One is about masculine energies and the other feminine ones. Some of the feminine energies are love, compassion, wisdom, caring, nurturing, contemplation and having an overall view. Some of the masculine energies are thinking, action, decision-making, providing and moving forward. The aim of the base chakra is to bring them into balance. When they work together in perfect harmony, energy flows freely up from your Earth Star and nurtures all the energies in your base.

Your base chakra is also where your beliefs about your material security are contained, so if there is an imbalance here, the centre will be tense and the base of your spine will become tight. This can block the flow of your prosperity.

An example of a balanced base chakra is when your masculine energy provides, while the feminine nurtures you, or when the masculine energy thinks, while the feminine adds wisdom. Then you have inner equilibrium and your base chakra relaxes.

Although unicorns hold the Divine Feminine, they are totally balanced, and when they pour light into your base chakra, it creates wholeness.

Kundalini

The kundalini, or life force, is sometimes likened to a snake curled up in the base chakra, ready to rise up through the spine as you waken to enlightenment. Another analogy is a seed waiting in the soil to sprout and grow as soon as conditions are right. This happens when you open up to higher frequencies. When you invite unicorn energy into your base chakra, it helps to enrich the compost there, so that the kundalini is perfectly nurtured and supported when it rises.

Saturn and Spiritual Discipline

The base chakra is where you learn and practise spiritual discipline. When you perfect it, you master and control all facets of your mind, emotions and body. The energy of spiritual discipline is being anchored in this universe from Quichy, the ascended aspect of Saturn. This is the foundation of your true power.

Great masters like St Germain and Merlin, who are the same soul, originate from Saturn. They developed the qualities of spiritual discipline and it enabled them to become incredible magicians and alchemists. St Germain achieved immortality and lived for 300 years as the Compte de St Germain to help the world. For centuries, he was master of the Seventh Ray, the Violet Ray of ceremonial order, magic and ritual. Now he serves on the Intergalactic Council and is Lord of Civilization, one of the highest offices in this universe. He is also one of the nine masters of Saturn.

Thanks to St Germain, the qualities of spiritual discipline are coded into your fifth-dimensional base chakra, which is your foundation for higher enlightenment and illuminated mastery.

Unicorn energy helps raise the frequency of the base chakra and anchor it to Saturn and its ascended aspect, Quichy, so that you can access the codes and bring them back to your base chakra to be activated. When you have done so, you experience total faith and bliss, for these are the rewards of mastery.

ANCHORING YOUR BASE CHAKRA TO SATURN

~ Find a space where you can be undisturbed.

~ Stroke down your spine with your breath and allow the base of your spine to relax.

~ See your base chakra as a platinum ball and notice how large it is.

~ Archangel Gabriel, in his pure white light, is standing beside you.

~ He places a yin-yang symbol of perfect balance in your base chakra.

~ Relax as you sense it bringing everything into equilibrium.

~ Your unicorn creates a ball of shimmering translucent white light for you and places it in your base chakra.

~ It enables a flow of light to reach out to Saturn.

~ You travel with your unicorn up the link to Saturn, where eight of the great masters of Saturn, dressed in black robes and wearing golden crowns, await.

~ They welcome you and conduct you through a light portal into Quichy, the ascended aspect of Saturn.

~ Here the ninth great master of Saturn, St Germain, awaits, radiating violet and platinum light.

~ He examines your aura and your life, then asks if you are ready to embrace spiritual discipline.

~ If you are, he nods.

~ He plunges a rod of violet fire down your spine into your base chakra, then touches your third eye. Notice how this feels.

~ Thank him and return to your base chakra on your unicorn.

~ Notice if the kundalini energy in your base has grown.

~ Nurture it in any way that feels right to you.

~ See the codes of light from Quichy lighting up in this chakra and know that new powers are being activated.

CHAPTER **32**

Unicorns and
the Sacral Chakra

The sacral centre is one of humanity's most challenging ones. The sacral and navel are two separate chakras encompassed within one large one and in the overall care of Archangel Gabriel. Both the sacral and the navel have 16 chambers, embraced within a 33rd one.

Like all our chakras, the sacral is on its own ascension journey. Ultimately, it is about transcendent love.

The Shadow of the Sacral Chakra

Those who are stuck or blocked in the first five chambers of the sacral chakra are emotionally needy and unfulfilled. They use sexuality for control or manipulation, e.g. child porn or stalking or being in a powerful position and misusing that power sexually, but they often feel powerless themselves. They need to be aligned to the heart chakra. Currently, a huge wave of light is being directed to humanity from the spiritual realms to bring this shadow to the surface and to raise the frequency of this chakra. Angelic beings like unicorns cannot bring their energy down that low, so it may be more appropriate to ask dragons to clear out the stickiness of the collective sacral and release the darkness so that unicorns can transmute it.

The next four chambers of the sacral chakra are where people are seeking emotional balance, but fear commitment or need to be the centre of attention. These are the chambers that often cause the downfall of people who are highly evolved in their other centres.

Genuine Caring

When the sacral starts to develop, it glows, and as you step through into the following chambers, you have an instinctive desire to help and befriend others from a genuine space of caring.

The final chamber is about supporting a baby into incarnation. In the Golden Age of Atlantis the entire extended family often meditated to discover what kind of soul they could best serve. It was understood that it was the privilege, honour and spiritual task of the whole community to look after a child. So, you may have no children of your own, but if you still need to learn the lesson of this chamber and have not already done so in other lives, an opportunity will certainly be presented to you to care for a child!

Transcendent Love

When this chakra is fully fifth-dimensional, it shimmers with the pale translucent pink of transcendent love. At this point, when you have learned the lessons of all the sacral chambers, your relationships, your family life and your sexuality all glow with harmony. When a unicorn touches this chakra, the light there explodes with higher love and joy, and a higher, purer element is added to your relationships, for the unicorn energy brings in pure Christ Light.

Sirius and Lakumay

The cosmic sacral chakra is Sirius and its ascended aspect, Lakumay. Here are held the keys and codes of the Christ Light and also the spiritual science and technology of the future. When your personal sacral chakra and Sirius are connected, you download keys and codes to help the planet forward. When you connect to Lakumay, you receive the grace of the Christ Light.

Quan Yin

Quan Yin, the great Chinese goddess, High Priestess and dragon master, is very connected to this chakra and works on the inner planes to pour her ineffable pink love into relationships.

CONNECTING WITH SIRIUS AND LAKUMAY

~ Find a place where you can relax and be undisturbed.

~ Focus on your sacral chakra and see it as a ball of pink energy.

~ Enter it and be aware of its 16 chambers. Notice if any person or attachments need to be cleared out or released.

~ Invoke your unicorn and relax as it pours pure white light into the chambers.

~ Feel or sense the chambers lighting up.

~ Anything you are ready to remove is being spun out.

~ Send light out from your sacral to Sirius and its ascended aspect, Lakumay.

~ Travel with your unicorn to Lakumay.

~ The beautiful Quan Yin awaits in a gentle shimmering pink light.

~ She and the unicorn merge their light and access ninth-dimensional Christ Light from the golden globe there.

~ They enfold you in the pink, white and gold light of transcendent love. Breathe it in.

~ They are wakening you to higher love.

~ Finally your unicorn returns with you to your sacral chakra and you fill it with codes of love.

CHAPTER 33

Unicorns and
the Navel Chakra

As outlined in the last chapter, the navel and the sacral chakras each contain 16 chambers with lessons to learn and assimilate, they are both within one huge chamber, the 33rd, and Archangel Gabriel is in charge of them both.

The bright orange navel is one of the transcendent chakras that was withdrawn at the fall of Atlantis. As you become fifth-dimensional again, this glorious centre is returned to you. It represents all the qualities of oneness, spiritual community and creativity.

Oneness

When a unicorn adds its light to your navel chakra, it opens you up to an enlightened perspective on the world. You see the common good in humanity and the best in those who are different from you. Unicorn light in this chakra accelerates the journey to oneness and will enable people everywhere to accept that they are all part of a single entity. When you know this, you realize you cannot harm yourself or anyone else without harming the whole and you cannot injure anyone else without injuring yourself. You know that when you respect and honour others, you respect and honour yourself.

An understanding of oneness is one of the great gifts of Lemuria.

Spiritual Community

In the Golden Era of Atlantis, people lived in communities that had common aims, and these are all encoded in our navel chakra now, waiting to be illuminated for the new Golden Age.

The Atlanteans lived in a constant state of gratitude to Source and this enabled them to attract abundance. They always acted for the highest good of the whole. They never received without giving or gave without receiving. This enabled a continuous flow of giving and receiving to happen and therefore no karma was created.

When faced with a decision, the community attuned to a higher power or Source to discover what was the best thing to do. Because the aim of everyone was to serve the highest good, there was no ego and the highest good revealed itself. There was always agreement, so everyone lived in harmony and peace.

Spiritual community meant the masculine and feminine were honoured equally. Everyone was encouraged to do what made their heart sing and gave them soul contentment. People were happy. Babies and children were considered special treasures and their welfare was the highest priority. All babies were anticipated and welcomed, so everyone felt wanted and loved. They spent much time out in nature, enjoying family and leisure pursuits. They ate locally grown, nutritious food, so they glowed with health. They expressed their creativity in many ways, and this was honoured.

Creativity

In the Golden Era of Atlantis, creativity was considered to be an expression of gratitude to Source. People loved to paint, especially abstracts in glowing colours. They made music, sang, danced, carved, played games and expressed themselves in every possible way. They put on exhibitions and shows. They had fun, and unicorns watched and added their light.

The navel chakra is the creative chakra. It is also the place where the Atlanteans envisioned their dreams and aims. These pictures were then raised to the Soul Star chakra, which radiated out the energy to manifest them. This powerful form of manifestation is being reactivated on Earth as people are once more being trusted to use the power for the highest good. When unicorns add their purity, grace and Divine Feminine wisdom to the navel chakra, it brings forward individual and collective higher visions.

The Sun and the Stargate of Helios

The navel chakra of this universe is our Sun, which is an ascended star holding the codes of the Divine Masculine. Divine Masculine energy is about leadership with integrity, force for the highest good and action with pure intention and peace. The Sun also holds the codes of happiness. Unicorns are ready to add their light to your navel chakra so that you can access these incredible codes for the golden future.

Helios, the Great Central Sun, is the Stargate to another universe through which Archangel Metatron pours his light. It then blazes directly through our Sun to us on Earth.

ACCESSING THE CODES OF THE SUN AND HELIOS

~ Find a place where you can be relaxed and undisturbed.

~ Place your attention on your navel chakra and sense it radiating orange, as if it were your personal Sun.

~ Be aware of Archangel Gabriel embracing this chakra, enabling it to hold steady and expand.

~ Your unicorn and Archangel Gabriel are pouring diamond light into the centre so it radiates out.

~ See the connection being formed between your navel and the Sun.

~ Ride on your unicorn along this light until you see the mighty Archangel Metatron, glowing golden orange, waiting for you.

~ Archangel Metatron greets you with a shaft of incredible love into your heart.

~ He invites you to sit on a blazing golden throne in the heart of the Sun.

~ And then he opens the doorway to Helios, so that a burst of sacred fire engulfs you.

~ For an instant you are one with the Infinite Sun.

~ And then your unicorn brings you back to your navel chakra.

~ He ignites the keys and codes of the Divine Masculine, spiritual community, higher creativity, happiness, manifestation and oneness within your navel.

~ Rest and relax as you integrate the new possibilities.

CHAPTER 34

Unicorns and
the Solar Plexus Chakra

Archangel Uriel is in charge of the development of the solar plexus chakras of all beings. This centre contains 33 chambers or lessons, which range from overcoming aggression and cowardice to having confidence, standing up for yourself and other people, and gaining inner peace and ultimately wisdom. It is the centre of your instincts and gut reactions. It is also a very delicate psychic centre that can hold on to emotional, mental and physical shocks and traumas. Unicorns will help you to heal these.

When this chakra is third-dimensional, it sends out antennae to sense for danger. In the fifth-dimensional paradigm, those fingers reach out with trust and wisdom to seek the best outcome to situations. As this develops, individuals as well as whole communities will start to have more confidence in themselves. When unicorns illuminate this chakra, it can expand enormously and bring inner peace to people and society as a whole. Over the next 20 years, this will rapidly spread peace throughout the Earth.

When the wisdom in everyone's solar plexus
emerges, world peace must happen.

Ascended Earth, Pilchay

The solar plexus of the universe is planet Earth. Earth has not yet ascended fully, but part of it has, and that aspect is called Pilchay. Unicorns can help to establish the connection between your solar plexus and Pilchay. The link goes down through your chakra column into the Golden Crystal Pyramid of Hollow Earth, the seventh-dimensional chakra in the centre of the planet, and moves through it into Pilchay. There all the wisdom that Earth has ever gained is stored and becomes available to you.

Here are the keys and codes of some of the special qualities that Lady Gaia and the unicorns can light up for you as you link directly to Pilchay.

Harmlessness

On this plane of free will, one of the highest-frequency qualities you can profess is harmlessness. When you are totally harmless in thought, word, emotion or act, every being around you feels safe and you yourself attract total safety. This solar plexus quality makes Earth and its ascended aspect, Pilchay, beloved throughout the universes.

Interdependence

Dependence is third-dimensional, independence fifth. However, when unicorns light up the codes of interdependence in your solar plexus, you hold the keys to the higher spiritual communities of the ascended universe.

Trust

When you trust that the spirit worlds and angelic realms will support you, they automatically respond to you and you are totally protected and looked after. All good things come your way and the golden light of true trust radiates from your solar plexus.

Intergalactic Mastery and Wisdom

When your solar plexus chakra is fully open, its lessons learned and its chambers activated, you become a wise one, a master. When unicorn blessings are added to this chakra, you become an intergalactic master, recognized throughout the universe.

BRINGING WHOLENESS TO YOUR SOLAR PLEXUS CHAKRA WITH UNICORNS

~   Find a place where you can relax and be undisturbed.

~   Gently rub your solar plexus and breathe comfortably into it.

~   Imagine it is a golden sunflower with 33 petals. See them open wide.

~ You may notice that some of the petals are bruised, torn or otherwise damaged. Call in your unicorn and ask it to pour the healing balm of its pure light into the centre of the sunflower.

~ See the petals become radiant and whole.

~ Your solar plexus is radiating golden fifth-dimensional light at this moment.

CONNECTING TO HOLLOW EARTH
AND PILCHAY WITH UNICORNS

~ Find a place where you can relax and be undisturbed.

~ Breathe peace and wisdom into your solar plexus until it relaxes.

~ Allow your unicorn to pour pure white light into it so that it becomes a scintillating golden-white ball.

~ Travel with your unicorn in the golden-white light as it moves down your chakra column into your Earth Star chakra.

~ Ride down together through roots into the beautiful world of Hollow Earth.

~ As you stand within the paradise of Hollow Earth, you connect with every animal, bird, human or other creature that has ever been on Earth.

~ Feel the interconnectedness. Experience the harmlessness and interdependence of all. Absorb these qualities.

~ Now enter the Golden Crystal Pyramid.

~ Lady Gaia, in luminous blue-green and rainbow colours, stands there and you enter her heart.

~ She opens a wonderful golden portal, shimmering with all the jewels of Earth.

~ You step through it into Pilchay, the ascended aspect of Earth, Lady Gaia's higher heart.

~ Lady Gaia enfolds you as you stand in the centre of this sacred inner world.

~ In a brilliant flash your unicorn illuminates the knowledge and wisdom acquired on Earth's journey.

~ You see the interconnectedness and interdependence of the entire universe.

~ For an instant you become one with All That Is.

~ And you are once more focused on your solar plexus, which is alight with extraordinary keys and codes and treasure.

~ Sit quietly and absorb this as you recognize who you truly are.

CHAPTER 35

Unicorns and
the Heart Chakra

The heart chakra is the spiritual centre of love. When it vibrates at the fifth-dimensional frequency, it becomes pure white with a little pink. It contains 33 chambers or petals, which take you on a journey to learn about the different aspects of love. Archangel Chamuel and his twin flame, Archangel Charity, are in charge of the development of the heart chakras of humanity, and unicorns are now working very closely with them.

As your heart chakra becomes fifth-dimensional, it expands and gets brighter. When unicorns add their light to it, it glows pure white and radiates such love that fingers of agape flow out from it to touch people and animals, who then feel actively loved and embraced by you.

The Journey of the Heart Chakra

The heart chakra is the most psychic of all the centres. In the Golden Era of Atlantis, every individual had a wide-open, totally blazing heart! They all reached out energetically from their heart centre to understand others without any intention of taking on their feelings. This enabled them to be one with another person without any emotional clouding.

For the last 10,000 years, human love has been very much about ego, so relationships have been based on neediness and dependency. You experience the ego aspects of emotions towards others in the first 10 chambers of the heart chakra. Only in the later chambers does your heart open to loving and caring for others and nature without any ego involvement.

Even the quality of empathy, which is a vibration that enables you to understand and share the feelings of another so that you become energetically one for a moment, is only the 18th lesson on the journey. When unicorns are invited to pour their light into this chamber, it enables you to step easily into the next one, the 19th, which offers the lesson of compassion, which is very similar, but more advanced. This is when you feel for another, but you stand apart and do not merge with their feelings. You are psychically attuned to others without taking in their energy.

After this, the following chambers take you through different lessons about forgiveness. Forgiveness is about opening your heart to love, no matter what another person has done. It is a very high-frequency quality that heals both giver and receiver, emotionally and physically. Humanity as a whole is currently being presented with these lessons, so that individuals as well as nations can become warmer and more welcoming towards others. By 2032, the heart chakras of all will have opened more and countries will be ready to be generous and to give unconditionally to their neighbours. Every time you ask unicorns to pour their light and blessings over the world, you are enabling the heart centres of all the people on the planet to open wider.

The last four chambers of the heart chakra take you through lessons about transcendent love, connection with the Cosmic Heart, universal love and finally oneness. When you are ready to open these doors wide, unicorns become very active around you, encouraging you fully to embrace oneness.

The Cosmic Heart

The heart chakra of the cosmos is Venus, which has ascended. This planet receives 12th-dimensional love directly from Source and steps it down to a frequency we can cope with on Earth. Every single time you visualize yourself in the Cosmic Heart, your personal heart receives a boost of light.

Angel Mary and Unicorn Energy

Angel Mary is a vast aquamarine Universal Angel, an archangel whose loving influence spreads throughout this universe and extends to others. She works directly with unicorn energy, and unicorns can always be present in the Cosmic Heart. Angel Mary is pure love.

OPENING YOUR HIGHER HEART

Here are six steps that enable you to open your higher heart chakra:

~ Merge yourself spiritually with open-hearted, high-frequency beings like Jesus, Quan Yin or Buddha. Their love consciousness will transmute your lower energies and open the chambers of your higher heart.

~ Invoke Archangels Chamuel and Charity and breathe their energy into your heart.

~ Invoke Archangel Mary and unicorns and immerse yourself in their light.

~ Constantly focus on oneness. Remember that at the higher levels there is no separation between you and every other person, animal or plant on this planet.

~ Visit the Cosmic Heart in meditations and sleep.

~ Ask unicorns to fill your heart with higher love by touching you with their horn of light.

CONNECTING TO THE COSMIC HEART WITH UNICORNS

~ Find a place where you can relax and be undisturbed.

~ Breathe into your heart chakra until you feel comfortable.

~ Sense or see your heart centre with its spiral of 33 chambers.

~ Take yourself on a walk round the spiral and notice the doors that are open or closed.

~ Then call in unicorns and ask them to pour light into your heart chakra.

~ See your heart opening and blazing love and higher understanding.

~ The unicorns and Archangel Chamuel are sending a shaft of light to Venus.

~   You travel with them into the heart of the Cosmic Heart, which is warm and welcoming and embraces you.

~   Angel Mary and the unicorns enfold you in a soft aquamarine-white cocoon of pure love and oneness.

~   Rest here as your heart is healed of the Earth experience and opened to transcendent love.

~   When you are ready, return to where you started from and live in love.

CHAPTER 36

Unicorns and
the Throat Chakra

The throat chakra is a high-frequency, very sensitive centre with 22 petals, dedicated to communication with truth. Its development is overseen by Archangel Michael and his twin flame, Faith. It is important to call in Archangel Michael's deep blue cloak of protection when you work there, until you have learned all its early lessons.

Developing this chakra encourages pure communication, for the qualities of the higher throat chakra are truth, honesty, integrity, honour and justice. To open it to its full potential, you must walk your talk.

The first of the chambers contains lessons about lying to protect yourself. Often people persuade themselves that they are telling untruths to shield their children or partners or employees, whereas they are in fact safeguarding themselves. When you deliberately tell a falsehood or let yourself be influenced by others, this inevitably has a dissonance, so people don't really trust you. Many politicians and big business leaders are wrestling with this, and bringing unicorn energy into this chakra will dramatically assist the honesty and trust levels throughout the planet.

The Throat Chakra Wound of Atlantis

One of the ancient wounds of Atlantis is the fear of being misunderstood, disbelieved or persecuted. For many lightworkers, this emotion has been exacerbated by lifetime after lifetime when healers and wise ones were oppressed for their knowing. This is the sixth lesson of this chakra. Like any fear, it leaves the chamber vulnerable to invasion by lower energies and this can bring the vibration of the whole throat centre down. This wound plays up when it is ready to be inspected and released. It is time now to heal it for everyone in the world. Calling in unicorns to fill this sixth chamber with their healing light can raise its frequency and heal the pain of the original wound.

Speaking Your Truth

As you move through the higher chambers of the throat chakra, you recognize who you are and accept your magnificence. You speak your truth and use your power to speak up for yourself and others with integrity. Then your throat chakra starts to radiate royal-blue light. Your unicorn is with you and you are ready to connect to Mercury, the throat chakra of the universe. The ascended aspect of Mercury is Telephony. Archangel Faith's energy is there and is really important in holding your intentions high and steady.

Inspired Leadership

When you become stronger and are clearer about who you really are and truly aligned with your divine self, you become a teacher of truth, an inspirational leader and an ambassador for Source. You trust yourself, and the door of the final throat chakra chamber opens when you totally trust God. Then your throat chakra blazes royal blue and gold and you inspire many people with your presence alone. Your unicorn is then ready to connect you to the stars and the angels of the Golden Ray.

Telepathy

Everyone is telepathic to some extent. In fact, most people are much more telepathic than they realize. It's not just about receiving clear messages from a friend or knowing who is phoning you before you answer the call; you constantly pick up the thoughts of others. Someone only has to think a critical or judgemental thought about you and your throat chakra will intuit it. Immediately and automatically your heart chakra will put up protection, without you even being aware of it. If someone sends you loving, admiring, respectful thoughts, on the other hand, your heart chakra will respond by opening a little.

When your throat chakra is completely open, you will know what others are feeling and thinking without even tuning in to the streams of their thoughts.

On an inner level you know everything,
for the psychic antennae from the throat
chakra are attuned to truth.

Mercury and Its Ascended Aspect, Telephony

Your personal throat chakra is connected to the planet Mercury, which is the throat chakra of this universe. Its ascended aspect is Telephony. I remember my sense of wonder and fascination when Kumeka first told me its name and I realized that the scientists who named the telephone must have been very well tuned in.

When you connect to Mercury, you receive codes of light in your throat chakra. When you reach Telephony, the high frequency there enables you to develop pure communication with all life forms and you start to communicate telepathically with the masters and angels on the Golden Ray. This is the ray of pure wisdom and love. Unicorns help by sending their light into your throat chakra to facilitate this connection.

The powers of the throat chakra also include levitation, teleportation, telekinesis and is the ability to send healing by the use of powerful thoughts, which many lightworkers are already doing. From this chakra, you radiate a magnificent royal blue and gold, lit with the diamond white of unicorn energy. You speak with majesty, truth, integrity and power for the highest good. You become one of Archangel Michael's warriors on Earth.

CONNECTING TO THE THROAT CHAKRA WITH UNICORNS

~   Find a place where you can be undisturbed.

~   Breathe deep-blue light into your throat chakra, relaxing and protecting it.

~ Ask Archangel Michael to touch your throat chakra with his Sword of Truth.

~ Find yourself walking through its chambers.

~ Notice which doors are closed (if any) and which doors are open.

~ Check whether or not there are any wounds remaining from Atlantis or any other lifetimes.

~ Ask your unicorn to fill your throat chakra with pure white healing light. Sense it happening.

~ And now your unicorn lights up your chambers of truth, integrity and honour.

~ Fly with your unicorn up a shaft of light to Mercury.

~ Then move through a portal surrounded by golden angels into Telephony.

~ Here the High Master of Telephony places a royal-blue and gold cloak over your shoulders.

~ Your unicorn then ignites the codes of truth in your throat.

~ Together you return down the shaft of light.

~ Focus again on your throat chakra and telepathically send messages of empowerment, healing and love to people everywhere.

~ When you are ready, open your eyes.

CHAPTER 37

Unicorns and
the Third Eye Chakra

The third eye is a very important chakra and many people want to open it to achieve clairvoyance or even total enlightenment. Unicorns can help you explore its 96 petals or chambers more quickly than you could otherwise do and at a rate that is comfortable and safe for you.

Archangel Raphael, the great emerald angel of healing and abundance, is in charge of the development of this chakra. When it becomes fifth-dimensional, it becomes crystal clear, rather like your own personal crystal ball.

Drugs, alcohol and heavy food clog this chakra, because it is so sensitive. The reverse is true, too, for it responds quickly to beautiful thoughts, light food and pure water.

With 96 lessons to learn in this centre, it may seem a huge task to open all its petals. However, when the Sun of happiness and warmth shines onto a flower, it starts to open naturally and quickly. The light of high intentions works in the same way for the third eye chakra!

The first chambers in its spiral take you through lack of awareness, spiritual blindness and refusal to see spirit. Anyone reading this will be well past that stage. You move on through accepting spirit to understanding and applying the laws of the universe. Then you must practise the right use of thoughts. Eventually you will reach expanded vision, abundance consciousness, higher perception and the blazing light of total enlightenment.

The rewards of this journey are abundance, perfect health, success and clairvoyance. Then your crystal ball is truly clear and polished.

Your unicorn can pour white light into your third eye chakra or it can send you crystal-clear transparent light. Either will enable you to accelerate the development of this chakra in a safe way. They also boost it, so that you can connect to the third eye chakra of the universe, which is Jupiter, and its ascended aspect, Jumbay.

Universal Angel Mary

Archangel Raphael's twin flame is the Angel Mary, a vast Universal Angel who spreads love in many universes. If asked, she will touch your third eye chakra with her pale aquamarine light of love and healing. This is especially significant, as she works very closely with unicorns. When they work together on your third eye chakra, you can expect magic to happen.

Abundance Consciousness

I receive more requests for help with money and prosperity of every sort than any others. Prosperity is part of abundance and the answers all lie within the beliefs you hold in your third eye chakra. We are all currently dealing with family and ancestral beliefs, as well as those from our own soul journey. Unicorn light flowing into this centre can raise its frequency enough to dissolve old unhelpful patterns.

Enlightenment

When all 96 chambers of your third eye chakra are fully open and the lessons learned, you are a fully enlightened master. You see everything from a high, wide, divine perspective and you know there is only love. When asked, unicorns will pour their light into this chakra to accelerate this process. They can help you dissolve the Veils of Illusion over your third eye (*see pages 164–167*). This all assists the path to enlightenment.

Perfect Health Blueprint

Archangel Raphael holds your perfect health blueprint in your third eye chakra. This is revealed on your journey through the chakra and unicorns will send in their special light to help bring it forward.

Clairvoyance

The third eye is also the chakra of inner seeing. But it is unwise to do third eye opening or kundalini-raising practices that force its opening, for you may open a doorway to a world of illusion. Some people who see into lower dimensions, especially under the influence of drugs or alcohol, find it a disturbing or frightening experience.

True clairvoyance means clear vision with the inner eye into other dimensions. At the advanced levels of clairvoyance, you may see divine colours or beings of the spiritual realms. Such experiences are pure, vivid, clear and inspirational. They carry the resonance of truth.

One of the gifts of unicorns is help with developing clairvoyance in a safe and gentle way.

Jupiter and Jumbay

Jupiter is the third eye chakra of the universe. It holds the keys and codes of happiness for every being in the cosmos.

Its ascended aspect, Jumbay, is about expansion, huge abundance, great happiness and success beyond your wildest dreams. When your unicorn helps you to attune to Jumbay, it enables the energy of unimaginable possibilities to pour into you.

CONNECTING TO JUPITER AND JUMBAY WITH UNICORNS

~ Find a place where you can be undisturbed.

~ Gently rub your forehead or breathe into it.

~ Ask your unicorn to journey with you round the spiral within your third eye.

~ Let it gently touch any closed doors to open them and pour light into any that need help.

~ Then let it fill the entire centre with pure transparent light.

~ See your third eye become a radiant crystal ball.

~ Travel with your unicorn through the universe to Jupiter, then into the vastness of Jumbay.

~ Archangel Raphael awaits you there in crystal green.

~ He invites you to view the universe from an enlightened perspective.

~ You see there is only love and abundance.

~ Then you see keys and codes of happiness, success, enlightenment, expansion, abundance and prosperity flowing down through a shaft of light into your third eye.

~ You travel back with your unicorn into the expanded crystal ball of your brow chakra.

~ Allow the keys and codes to create new beliefs and patterns in this centre.

~ When you are ready, open your eyes.

CHAPTER 38

Unicorns and
the Crown Chakra

Archangel Jophiel, the angel of wisdom, is in charge of the development of the crown chakra. His twin flame, Archangel Christine, as her name suggests, adds Christ Light.

The thousand petals of the crown chakra are designed to unfurl and reach out into the universe to access cosmic knowledge and wisdom when you are ready for them. As the crystal-clear fifth-dimensional chakra opens, some points in the crown will start to connect to illumined cosmic energies.

Cosmic Connections

Your soul may already have linked with certain stars, planets or great energies in other lifetimes. You may be making more connections in this one while you are asleep or during meditation. When you invite your unicorn to pour its light into your crown chakra, these universal links become purer and clearer. What might you access?

Pools and Flames of Light from Golden Atlantis

These great Atlantean energies are now carefully positioned round the universe and you can access them. They include the Mahatma energy, the White Ascension Flame of Atlantis, the Aquarian Ascension Pool, the Cosmic Diamond Violet Flame and many others. Unicorn light and love are the glue that solidifies these connections.

Stars, Planets and Galaxies

Every star, planet and galaxy is a chakra, whether or not it is a main one or even one you have heard of. Each holds incredible light, knowledge and wisdom and carries special cosmic qualities. Unicorns are waiting to add their particular energies to the petals of your crown to enable your links to these cosmic bodies to be activated.

Numbers

Numbers out in the cosmos carry great powers. I describe these in Chapter10 (*see page 64*).

Sacred Geometric Symbols

Many of the sacred geometric symbols are powerful on Earth, but out in the universe they are enormously potent. Symbols like the Metatron Cube, the ankh, the cross, the diamond, the circle, the cube, the infinity symbol and others, including the pyramid, are vast power sources receiving light directly from Source. The crystal pyramids from the Dome of Atlantis, which are charged with pure Source energy, are waking up now and getting ready for us to access the knowledge and light programmed within them.

Becoming an Intergalactic Master

Whenever you make a galactic connection, it adds to the light in your crown chakra. This is then propelled up through your higher chakras and helps to build your Antakarana bridge to Source. Crossing the Antakarana is the journey to intergalactic mastery, a journey facilitated by unicorns and the Seraphim Seraphina.

Lord Voosloo

Lord Voosloo was the highest-frequency High Priest ever to incarnate in Atlantis and he activated the jump shift that enabled that civilization to become the one of legend. Previously, he helped the civilization of Mu to make the shift to ascension. He has now returned to help Earth make a similar leap into the new Golden Age. He works on the crystal sunshine Yellow Ray and can touch and expand your crown chakra so you can accelerate your journey to enlightenment and ascension.

Unicorns Pour Blessings onto the Crown Chakra

When unicorns see the petals of your crown opening, they pour blessings and showers of light over you. You can ask them to accelerate the opening process.

Uranus and Curonay

The cosmic crown chakra of the universe is Uranus and it enables you to connect with cosmic telepathy and higher communication. Originality, liberation, individuality, independence and leadership are also held there, as well as spiritual gifts and talents. Uranus holds a waiting space for all the possibilities of the future, the creative energies and as yet unimagined technological ideas that are ready to be brought to Earth as soon as the old, unwanted structures and patterns have been dissolved.

When enough people open their crown chakra, there will be massive social change and restructuring on a global scale.

Curonay is the ascended aspect of Uranus. When you connect to it, you connect to enormous possibilities for divine transformation and you will experience higher enlightenment. When everyone makes this connection, there will be a great leap in consciousness on the planet.

CONNECTING TO URANUS AND CURONAY WITH UNICORNS

~ Find a place where you can be undisturbed.

~ Sit with your back straight, close your eyes and relax.

~ Focus on the top of your head and see your crown chakra as a ball of transparent light.

~ Archangels Jophiel and Christine, in pale crystal yellow, are holding it steady.

~ Your unicorn pours a blessing of white light over it and the petals start to unfurl.

~ A great shaft of white light flies out to Curonay and you ride up it on your unicorn.

~   The great illumined master Lord Voosloo awaits you there and triggers a jump shift in your consciousness.

~   You sense the thousand petals of your crown expand and link into the great energies of the cosmos.

~   Your unicorn is constantly sending out light to encourage and enable this process.

~   You look down and see yourself connected to the entire universe. Absorb the feeling.

~   When you are ready, your unicorn takes you back to where you started from.

~   Thank it, knowing you have touched higher enlightenment.

CHAPTER 39

Unicorns and
the Causal Chakra

The causal chakra is above the crown and is a transcendent chakra that has always been fifth-dimensional. It used to lie slightly behind the other chakras and be contained within the head. The people of the Golden Era of Atlantis had elongated skulls to house it. It is now moving forward to be integrated into a column of light with the other chakras. This is another sign of humanity's spiritual progress.

All the centres other than the causal have several petals or chambers. However, the causal is one single huge chamber. It is through this chamber that you access the angelic realms. When your causal chakra is open and activated, you can connect with angels, dragons, unicorns and illumined ones. It also acts as your own personal Moon, pouring Divine Feminine energy over you.

The causal chakra is a single chamber for peace.
It is humans' entry to the angelic kingdoms.

Archangel Christiel

Archangel Christiel is in charge of the development of the causal chakras of humanity. He is a Universal Angel and is such a high-frequency being that he has only been able to enter this universe in the last few years, since the vibration of humanity rose. As his name suggests, he carries pure Christ Light. His twin flame is Archangel Mallory, who is a keeper of ancient wisdom and carries Divine Feminine light.

Archangel Christiel vibrates on the shimmering luminous Silver-White Ray and is an archangel of peace who spreads Christ Light. The ineffable peace he is already pouring onto Earth through the Moon is beginning to touch the masses with a desire for harmony and oneness.

The Moon

The Moon is the causal chakra of our universe and Archangel Christiel sends his light to it. It is where the frequency of the pure Divine Feminine light is stepped down for Earth.

I once saw Archangel Christiel's face when I was looking at the Full Moon. He only smiled at me for an instant, but it was a heart-stoppingly awesome moment and the memory of it remains with me.

The Stargate of Lyra

The highest-frequency unicorns live in another universe beyond the Stargate of Lyra, which is the 12th-dimensional energy portal they use to step into this universe. Archangel Christiel's energy is concentrated there and simply tuning in to it raises your frequency enormously.

The Unicorn Pathway

When Archangel Christiel sends a finger of light from the Stargate of Lyra through the Moon to Earth, it forms a pathway for unicorns. Many of them come down this route. They are then able to step into the causal chakras of people who are ready for them and enter the Earth.

You can serve the universe by preparing your causal chakra to allow unicorns to enter this planet. Some people allow thousands of unicorns to enter Earth through their causal centre. This is a huge act of devotion that raises the frequency of your causal and accelerates your ascension.

BRINGING UNICORNS TO EARTH THROUGH YOUR CAUSAL CHAKRA

~ Sit comfortably, knowing that unicorns are about to transform your entire life.

~ Find yourself in a beautiful valley in the Himalayan mountains, the purest part of the world.

~ You are resting near a waterfall cascading over rocks and ferns, watching sunlight sparkling on the water.

~ Mentally call in your unicorn and see a magnificent shimmering white horse approaching you.

~ Your heart energy connects like a firework exploding as you greet it.

~ You climb onto its back and feel safe and loved as you rise together.

~ Above you, you see the entrance to a cave. The unicorns lands on a ledge in front of it.

~ As you enter the cave, you discover, to your amazement, that it is a vast crystal cavern, lit by millions of flickering candles.

~ Together, you and your unicorn walk through this wonderland that seems to go deep into the mountain.

~ You become aware of a shaft of pure silver light ahead.

~ As you reach it, you discover there is a huge hole in the top of the cavern, aligned directly to the Full Moon.

~ Moonlight streams down over you and your unicorn. Bathe in it for a long moment.

~ The unicorn rises with you up the shaft of moonlight. It is taking you to Lyra.

~ At last you see the magnificent Stargate of Lyra above you, shimmering in the light.

~ You lean forward and touch it. It swings open.

~ Beyond the Stargate are hundreds of unicorns.

~ Among them, Archangel Christiel, in glowing pearl-white, awaits you.

~ He raises his hands and showers beautiful Christ Light over you.

~ With a gesture, he invites you to enter the unicorn kingdom.

~ You and your unicorn both move forward.

~ You find yourself in the midst of hundreds of shimmering unicorns. They surround you with love and pour divine blessings from their horns over you.

~ You are in a sea of unicorn light.

~ Archangel Christiel enfolds you in his vast soft wings and you look down through the Stargate at the Moon.

~ Archangel Christiel sends a glowing silver-white finger of energy down through the Moon to your causal chakra above your head on Earth.

~ And then you and your unicorn are flying along the glowing silver pathway of liquid light to the Moon, where you rest for a moment.

~ You are followed by thousands of unicorns.

~ You look down as the causal chakra above your head grows bigger, as if it were turning into your own Moon.

~ You all move from the Moon through the shimmering silver-white light to the causal chakra above your head.

~ You enter your causal, your own vast chamber of peace.

~ There is a door there to the angelic realms. It is open and you continue through it on your unicorn.

~ The light of the seventh heaven surrounds you and you look round to see how many unicorns are with you.

~ How many have stepped onto Earth through your causal chakra?

~ They surround you now, showering you with blessings.

~ Then you watch them spread out around the planet on their missions to help humanity.

~ And you thank your unicorn before opening your eyes.

CHAPTER 40

Unicorns and
the Soul Star Chakra

Your Soul Star chakra, in the charge of Archangel Mariel and his twin flame, Archangel Lavender, is a huge transcendent chakra containing 33 chambers. These contain all the records of your long soul journey. Also within this chakra is all the wondrous learning and experience you have accumulated, as well as the wisdom you have acquired. When your Soul Star is fully open and active, it is a luminous, clear magenta.

You start to connect with this chakra when you accept that you have a soul mission. It is divided into two sections. There is a lower part that contains lessons about accepting and loving yourself, your family and your community. Every parent or person in service is automatically presented with opportunities to learn these lessons. Archangel Zadkiel, the violet angel of transmutation, oversees this part of the Soul Star.

You then move into the upper section. Archangel Mariel and Archangel Lavender will guide you here. There is still more to clear, for in the first chambers all the karma and the family and ancestral undertakings that your soul has agreed to deal with in this lifetime are stored. You may well have done much clearing of family and ancestral lines. However, some experiences may be deeply entrenched and still impacting on you. For example, if you or one of your ancestors tangled with someone in the past and relentlessly refused to forgive or release, you will continue to be corded to that negative energy. It will remain a block in your soul records.

Archangel Lavender's role is to help you release these blocks and clear any remaining karma and unresolved ancestral energy. This gracious archangel can go down the lines of ancestors or people you have been involved with and soften their hearts with understanding and wisdom. Unicorns accompany her on this journey of service. They can also help dissolve old soul patterns, including family and ancestral ones held in this chakra.

Once this is complete, you gain access to the highest aspect of your Soul Star, where Archangel Mariel holds the light, and it becomes a spiritual centre of higher love, filled with Christ consciousness. It then connects with the Cosmic Heart and you access your past-life gifts, knowledge and wisdom.

When you reach this higher chamber, your frequency rises, and as unicorns add their magnificent light, your Higher Self is illuminated. Then you start the journey to merge with your Monad.

RECEIVING UNICORN SOUL HEALING

~ Find a place where you can be quiet and undisturbed.

~ Raise the frequency with sacred music, beautiful flowers or crystals, or another beautiful thing that appeals to you.

~ Sit or lie comfortably and ground yourself by visualizing your Earth Star chakra being rooted into the heart of Lady Gaia.

~ Find yourself by a bright turquoise lake that is perfectly reflecting the clear blue sky above you.

~ You are sitting on the white sand that fringes the lake.

~ Suddenly you notice shining coloured lights dancing round you and you realize these are fairies.

~ Flickering with excitement, they lead you to a huge flat quartz crystal that has been hidden by lavender bushes.

~ As you touch it, a strange thrill runs through you, like an electric current.

~ And at that moment your wondrous unicorn appears in front of you.

~ He invites you to lie on the crystal.

~ The fairies form a shimmering ring of coloured lights around you.

~ The unicorn pours a blessing of a trillion sparks like a fountain over you.

~ As they cascade over you, the entire crystal lights up with blue, pink, yellow and many other colours.

~ You can feel the energy pulsing through you.

~ And then the unicorn touches the top of your head with the light from its horn.

~ There is a moment of intense silence.

~ You find yourself between the upper and lower chambers of your Soul Star chakra.

~ Archangel Lavender, in a gentle lavender-coloured light, is holding her hand out to you. Your unicorn stands beside her.

~ You step between them and feel their light supporting you and lighting you up.

~ They lead you to a gateway and you see dozens of paths fanning out from it.

~ Archangel Lavender explains that these are your ancestral lines and past-life lines.

~ You follow Archangel Lavender and your unicorn down one of them. You may go a long way.

~ When you stop, you see figures, twisted and black with crystallized emotion. You may never have known these people, but their energy is corded into you.

~ With compassion, say that you are sorry you hurt them. Their hands are over their ears, so they cannot hear. But together Archangel Lavender and the unicorn pour such loving and Source-infused light over them that they stand upright, take their hands from their ears, open their eyes and see the light. Their hearts open and love flows between you.

~ The cords between you all dissolve. You are free. Feel it in your body.

~ Archangel Lavender and the unicorn take you to other beings like this until your karmic and ancestral lines are totally clear.

~ Feel yourself being washed by wave after wave of light.

~ And then Archangel Lavender leaves you.

~ The unicorn points to a golden staircase that has appeared in front of you. It leads to a massive diamond-studded doorway.

~ Climbing the staircase, you push open the door, which opens onto a beautiful and wondrous temple.

~ Archangel Mariel himself, a brilliant shimmering magenta light, is waiting for you, holding a golden key.

~ Many doors from this room lead to the gifts, knowledge and wisdom you have acquired during your long soul journey.

~ Archangel Mariel hands you the key and your unicorn follows you as you explore the beauty of your soul. Take as long as you like.

~ When you are ready, the unicorn takes you back to the huge healing crystal.

~ The fairies are waiting for you, holding the energy of your journey for you.

~ Mentally ask them to hold this light for you until everything is fully cleared and the new energy assimilated.

~ They joyfully agree. Thank them.

~ They take you by the hand and lead you back to the pure turquoise waters of the lake.

~ Here you bathe, symbolically clearing and cleansing yourself.

~ When you come out of the water, a pure white robe with a golden sash awaits you.

~ Put it on and know you are ready to walk a higher path.

~ Open your eyes with a smile.

CHAPTER 41

Unicorns and
the Stellar Gateway Chakra

The Stellar Gateway, your 12th chakra, houses the energy of your divine essence, the original spark from Source, and is a storehouse of all your experiences. It is literally the gateway to your Monad, your I AM Presence, your 12th-dimensional aspect.

Ascension Lift to the Stellar Gateway Portal

The crown chakra is the first centre through which you can connect to stellar energies. At this level, you feel you have ascended in the ascension elevator to a great height, and when you look out at the world, you see that you are way above it. You feel you can touch the stars. But the cosmic ascension lift can take you much higher. When you are ready, it allows you to access the Stellar Gateway chakra.

The vibration at the Stellar Gateway chakra is so incredible that it is beyond the understanding of most of us. It is as if you have explored each floor of your skyscraper and then you reach the 12th level and find yourself on the rooftop terrace. Out here, you are in touch with All That Is. You are at one with the wisdom and the oneness of the universe. There is absolutely no separation between you and everything there is. You have stepped into a portal among the stars. You are in the higher frequencies of the universe and unicorns are holding you in their light.

Two vast beings maintain the frequency of this chakra and prepare you to access the light of God. These are Archangel Metatron and the Seraphim Seraphina.

Archangel Metatron

This illumined golden orange archangel is one of the mightiest in the archangel realms. He is helping the whole of humanity to raise their vibration now. As soon as your lower chakras are ready, he enables the golden chalice of your Stellar Gateway, to open, like a cosmic flower, to receive Source light. He may also offer you his golden orange Metatron Cloak to protect you and help you maintain the frequencies of your fifth-dimensional chakras. He watches over your entire ascension journey.

Seraphina

The task of the wondrous Seraphim Seraphina is to help you build your Antakarana bridge from your Stellar Gateway to connect fully to your Monad and Source. Your Antakarana bridge is a spiritual ladder that takes you up through various initiations. When you reach a certain level, you are presented with a choice: you can either train in Seraphina's intergalactic schools to serve the universe by becoming an intergalactic master or you can take a direct but equally challenging path to Source. One path is not better than the other; they simply utilize different talents and skills that you have acquired during the long journey of your soul. Seraphina's task is to guide your footsteps along the right path for your soul.

Step into the Portal of the Stellar Gateway

If you are reading this, you have earned this opportunity to enter the Stellar Gateway portal by diligent spiritual practice over many lifetimes. For most humans, it takes several incarnations to access this ascension portal. This is why religious and spiritual lives were so prized in the past: they gave souls an opportunity to focus on their life quest without outside temptation and interference. Now, however, in this turbulent birthing period before the start of the new Golden Age, most lightworkers are undertaking their quest out in the world.

The reason for this is the great desire of awakened souls to help humanity despite the challenges and diversions of modern life. Those who have chosen to help the planet ascend are powerful. Even if you don't believe it, if you are reading this, unicorn energy is lighting your way so that you can step into the illuminated portal at the top of the ascension path and experience ultimate consciousness and oneness.

A breathtaking reward of oneness is Monadic claircognizance, cosmic all-knowing. You become part of an expanded universe and experience it at the level of the Stellar Gateway. And you automatically become a beacon. Your light shines into the inner planes, bringing hope, inspiration and comfort to everyone.

Expressing the Light of Your Stellar Gateway

Ascension is really about descension. You have taken the elevator to the 12th floor. It is alight with golden frequencies, experiences and wisdom. Now it is time for you to bring that amazing energy down and express it in your daily life.

Letting Go of Ego

The Stellar Gateway is the ultimate peace chamber. Whenever you lose your state of peace, serenity, tranquillity and harmlessness, it is because you are engaged with your ego. You are trying to control, or feel better than or not as good as another, or a million other feelings. Peace, serenity, tranquillity and harmlessness are the rewards of letting go of your negative ego.

If your soul wants to remind you of this, someone will certainly step into your environs to test you! As I was writing this, I had a huge awareness about my reaction to my teenage granddaughter, who decided to move in and live with me just as my house was on the market to be sold. I saw that I had attracted this as a test. Teenagers are not entirely compatible with keeping a home immaculate for people to view. I could feel my control hackles rising and this certainly disturbed my inner peace. But I realized that if I let go of my ego around this, I could keep the house reasonably tidy and attract the perfect buyer. It worked!

When you are connected to your golden self, you don't need to attract people who rattle your cage.

People use mantras, prayers, chants, meditation and a myriad of other spiritual practices to maintain their frequency and keep themselves focused on their goal of stepping into the portal of the Stellar Gateway. That is wonderful and really helpful. The most important spiritual practice of all, however, is dealing with the circumstances and people that come into your life.

Unicorns are drawn to pure, good,
generous, caring, heart-centred people
who ascend just by being themselves.

YOUR UNICORN AND THE STELLAR GATEWAY

~ Find a place where you can be undisturbed.

~ Find yourself in your Earth Star chakra, ready to step into an ascension lift.

~ Your unicorn pours blessings over you to light up your journey.

~ You enter the ascension lift and press number 12.

~ The lift rises through your Earth Star, base, sacral, navel, solar plexus, heart, throat, third eye, crown, causal and Soul Star chakras.

~ Finally you reach the top of the skyscraper. You reach your Stellar Gateway.

~ The doors of the elevator open and you are among the stars, at one with the universe.

~ The light is golden and Archangel Metatron approaches you in his magnificent golden orange cloak.

~ Beside him is the most awesome shimmering diamond-white unicorn you have ever seen.

~ Archangel Metatron greets you with love and joy.

~ He places his golden orange Metatron Cloak sprinkled with diamonds over you.

~ For an instant you are aware of who you truly are and the experiences you have had throughout the universes. You know you are a vast being.

~ The Seraphim Seraphina now approaches in robes of rainbow light and takes you to a golden bridge, stretching up out of sight.

~ She indicates it is your Antakarana bridge and you place your foot on the first step.

~ Seraphina places her wings around you, holding you steady and safe.

~ And then the entire bridge lights up and flashes, inviting you to ascend it. Move up as far as feels right.

~ You are bathing in the golden light of your Stellar Gateway and are open to universal downloads.

~ When you are ready, the diamond unicorn brings you back to where you started from.

CHAPTER 42

Unicorns Light Up Your
Sixth-Dimensional Chakras

In the Golden Era of Atlantis, only the High Priests and Priestesses could reach sixth-dimensional frequencies, and then only for a short period of time. How did they do it? The chakra column is like a ladder. When you are ready to bring down a higher range of chakras, the lower ones descend into the Earth and the new ones drop down to take their place. So the High Priests and Priestesses of that illumined age would pull their sixth-dimensional chakra column down into their body in order to do particular pieces of galactic work.

We are destined to move into a new Golden Age where the frequencies will be higher than they were in the Atlantean period. Tim Whild reminded me that during the Golden Era of Atlantis the planet itself was third-dimensional, so it was an awesome achievement for the humans on it to reach and maintain a fifth-dimensional frequency. By the time the new Golden Age of Aquarius is established, Earth itself will be fully fifth-dimensional and this will support us all in reaching higher vibrations. Already lightworkers are bringing in their sixth-dimensional chakras for a little while and this is enabling them momentarily to contact the 10th dimension. This is because we can reach up to four dimensions higher than the one in which we are at any given time.

In 2018, for the first time in 10,000 years, those who brought in their sixth-dimensional chakras could connect with awesome 10th-dimensional unicorns.

The Colours of the Sixth-Dimensional Chakras

In the sixth dimension, the colours of the chakras are much more ethereal and suffused with a gentle luminous silver light. They are changing constantly as individuals and humanity grow. These are the hues at the moment:

- The Earth Star chakra is a soft ethereal translucent silver.

- The base chakra radiates ethereal silver-platinum light.

- The sacral chakra radiates ethereal silver-pink light.

- The navel chakra radiates ethereal translucent silver-peach light.

- The solar plexus chakra radiates ethereal translucent golden light with silver shining through it.

- The heart chakra radiates ethereal translucent silver-white.

- The throat chakra radiates shimmering pale ethereal translucent blue.

- The third eye radiates shimmering ethereal translucent silver-green.

- The crown chakra radiates silver-yellow streams of light.

- The causal chakra radiates pale ethereal silver-white.

- The Soul Star chakra shimmers with ethereal translucent silver mauve-pink.

- The Stellar Gateway chakra pours out translucent crystal silver-gold.

When diamond unicorns add their
light to the sixth-dimensional chakras,
wonders and magic can happen.

ADDING 10TH-DIMENSIONAL UNICORN LIGHT TO YOUR SIXTH-DIMENSIONAL CHAKRAS

PREPARING A SPACE

For this special visualization it is essential that you are in an energetically high-frequency place. First make sure it is spotless both physically and energetically. To recap, here are some things you can do to ensure your space is sparkling clean:

~ Ask air dragons to blow out any lower vibrations and blow in higher ones.

~ Use singing bowls or cymbals to clear old energies.

~ Clap and 'om' into the corners. This breaks up stuck energy and replaces it with new.

~ Place amethyst crystals in the corners.

DRAWING DOWN YOUR SIXTH-DIMENSIONAL CHAKRAS

~ Find a place where you can be quiet and undisturbed.

~ Make sure your feet are on the ground.

~ Let yourself relax.

~ Close your eyes and breathe comfortably.

~ Sense your aura becoming brighter.

~ Above you, your sixth-dimensional chakras are waiting. They look like a ladder of ethereal colours.

~ See or sense unicorns round you, shimmering with pure white light.

~ Visualize your fifth-dimensional chakras starting to move down below your feet, allowing the higher-frequency ones to slide down into their place.

~ See the beautiful new chakras in place.

YOUR SIXTH-DIMENSIONAL EARTH STAR CHAKRA

~ Focus on your Earth Star, which is now a soft ethereal translucent silver.

~ A unicorn steps forward and adds its pure white light to it.

~ Your Earth Star lights up, expands and radiates luminous silver out to the universe.

~ The light touches Toutillay, the part of Neptune that has already ascended, then spreads out to touch all the planets with a message of love from Lady Gaia.

YOUR SIXTH-DIMENSIONAL BASE CHAKRA

~ Focus on your base chakra, which is now glowing with ethereal translucent silver-platinum light.

~ A unicorn steps forward and adds its pure white light to it. Your chakra blazes.

~ Your base chakra expands and radiates luminous silver-platinum out to the universe.

~ When the energy reaches Quichy, the aspect of Saturn that has ascended, the masters of Saturn bless it and unicorns take the energy of spiritual discipline and perfect balance to every star, planet and galaxy in the universe.

~ Then it returns, enhanced, to your base chakra.

YOUR SIXTH-DIMENSIONAL SACRAL CHAKRA

~ Focus on your sacral chakra, which is now shimmering with ethereal translucent silver-pink light.

~ A unicorn steps forward and adds its pure white light to it. Your chakra flares out.

~ Your sacral chakra radiates luminous silver-pink out to the universe.

~ When the light touches Lakumay, the aspect of Sirius that has ascended, transcendent love spreads from there round the universe.

~ Breathe this expanded love back into your sacral chakra.

YOUR SIXTH-DIMENSIONAL NAVEL CHAKRA

~ Focus on your navel chakra, which is now glittering with ethereal translucent silver-peach light.

~ A unicorn steps forward and adds its pure white light to it.

~ Your navel chakra expands and radiates luminous silver-peach.

~ It reaches the Sun and activates masculine power, which bursts forth into the cosmos.

~ Unicorns bring the power back into your navel chakra.

Your Sixth-Dimensional Solar Plexus Chakra

~ Focus on your solar plexus chakra, which is now emanating ethereal translucent gold with silver shining through it.

~ A unicorn steps forward and adds its pure white light to it.

~ Your solar plexus chakra expands and radiates luminous silver-gold out to the cosmos.

~ It gathers peace from the entire planetary system, then draws it back to Earth and its ascended aspect, Pilchay.

~ Breathe that cosmic peace into your solar plexus chakra.

Your Sixth-Dimensional Heart Chakra

~ Focus on your heart chakra, which is now radiating ethereal translucent silver-white.

~ A unicorn steps forward and adds its pure white light to it.

~ Your heart chakra expands and radiates luminous silver-white out to the universe.

~ When the light touches Venus, the Cosmic Heart, there is an explosion of higher love.

~ Millions of unicorns take this cosmic love everywhere it is needed, then pour it at an even higher frequency into your heart.

Your Sixth-Dimensional Throat Chakra

~ Focus on your throat chakra, which is now emitting shimmering ethereal translucent silver-blue.

~ A unicorn steps forward and adds its pure white light to it. Your chakra blazes electric-blue and white.

~ Your throat chakra expands and radiates luminous silver-blue out to Telephony, the ascended aspect of Mercury.

~ Thousands of unicorns take this light out to touch every part of the universe with higher communication and perfect integrity.

~ The light flows back into your throat chakra at an even higher frequency.

YOUR SIXTH-DIMENSIONAL THIRD EYE CHAKRA

~ Focus on your third eye, which is now emanating shimmering ethereal translucent silver-green.

~ A unicorn steps forward and adds a ball of pure white light to it.

~ Your third eye chakra expands and sends waves of luminous silver-green out to Jumbay, the part of Jupiter that has ascended.

~ Unicorns gallop in to take this light and spread higher enlightenment and abundance consciousness to the entire universe.

~ Then they bring it back into your third eye with new, higher enlightenment.

YOUR SIXTH-DIMENSIONAL CROWN CHAKRA

~ Focus on your crown chakra, on the top of your head, which is now releasing silver-yellow streams of light.

~ A unicorn steps forward and pours a cascade of pure white light over you.

~ Your crown chakra expands and each of the thousand spikes sends a luminous silver-yellow searchlight out into the universe, connecting with the stars.

~ As one of the beams reaches Curonay, the part of Uranus that has ascended, a trillion links radiate out, touching every star.

~ Unicorns hold this beautiful web of light before the energy returns into your crown to illuminate you with universal wisdom.

YOUR SIXTH-DIMENSIONAL CAUSAL CHAKRA

~ Focus on your causal chakra, your own personal Moon above your head, which is now glowing ethereal translucent silver-white.

~ A unicorn steps forward and adds its pure white light to it.

~ Your causal chakra expands and beams luminous silver-white out to the Moon.

~ Unicorns spread this Divine Feminine peace energy round the cosmos. Then they return it, enhanced, to your causal chakra.

YOUR SIXTH-DIMENSIONAL SOUL STAR CHAKRA

~ Focus on your Soul Star chakra, which is now shimmering with ethereal translucent silver mauve-pink.

~ A unicorn steps forward and adds a stream of pure white light to it.

~ Your Soul Star chakra expands and bursts like a firework, sending luminous silver mauve-pink exploding out to Orion.

~ Unicorns blow this higher love and wisdom everywhere.

~ Sense it returning into your Soul Star and see the chakra become vast.

YOUR STELLAR GATEWAY CHAKRA

~ Focus on your Stellar Gateway chakra, which is now a great ethereal golden orange chalice pouring out translucent crystal silver-gold.

~ The brightest diamond-white unicorn steps forward and adds its pure clear light to it.

~ Your Stellar Gateway chakra glows and radiates luminous silver-gold out to Nigellay, the ascended aspect of Mars, the cosmic Stellar Gateway.

~ This light, brighter than any you have ever seen, radiates out to the universe.

~ Amazing high-frequency unicorns add this light to your Antakarana bridge, extending it to your Monad and Source.

~ Feel the connection.

YOUR SIXTH-DIMENSIONAL INTEGRATED CHAKRAS

~ Be aware that your chakras have become a column of radiant silver rainbow light. You are glowing and shimmering like a trillion stars.

~ Your energy reaches out to the heavens and you are part of the great cosmic web of light.

~ And now you are ready to experience a 10th-dimensional frequency. Be aware of an unbelievably bright white energy approaching.

~ An ineffable 10th-dimensional unicorn steps out of it and touches you with its horn.

~ You ignite like a thousand-watt bulb. Your light can be seen from the heavens.

~ Spend as long as you need absorbing this frequency.

~ Then open your eyes, knowing that you have been truly blessed.

*Fly with unicorns and they will take you into
the pure realms of truth and divine love.*

Conclusion

Throughout this book, unicorns have connected more and more closely with you. They help you see life from the highest perspective. This is enlightenment.

Here is a message from them:

You have incarnated now to be a midwife for the new Golden Age and we have arrived in force to help you during Earth's challenging birthing process. We bring a message of hope. Be patient, for a golden future lies ahead. We will touch you with hope, grace, inspiration, trust, faith and all the other qualities you need to live in the wonderful new world we promise.

Call us and we will be there for you.

ABOUT THE AUTHOR

Diana Cooper received an angel visitation during a time of personal crisis. She is now well known for her work with angels, Orbs, Atlantis, unicorns, ascension and the transition to the new Golden Age. Through her guides and angels she enables people to access their spiritual gifts and psychic potential, and also connects them to their own angels, guides, Masters and unicorns. Diana is the founder of The Diana Cooper Foundation, a not-for-profit organization that offers certificated spiritual teaching courses throughout the world. She is also the bestselling author of 34 books, which have been published in 28 languages.

www.dianacooper.com

Free e-newsletters from Hay House, the Ultimate Resource for Inspiration

Be the first to know about Hay House's free downloads, special offers, giveaways, contests, and more!

 Get exclusive excerpts from our latest releases and videos from *Hay House Present Moments*.

 Our *Digital Products Newsletter* is the perfect way to stay up-to-date on our latest discounted eBooks, featured mobile apps, and Live Online and On Demand events.

 Learn with real benefits! *HayHouseU.com* is your source for the most innovative online courses from the world's leading personal growth experts. Be the first to know about new online courses and to receive exclusive discounts.

 Enjoy uplifting personal stories, how-to articles, and healing advice, along with videos and empowering quotes, within *Heal Your Life*.

Sign Up Now!

Get inspired, educate yourself, get a complimentary gift, and share the wisdom!

Visit www.hayhouse.com/newsletters to sign up today!

HAY
HOUSE

HAYHOUSE
online learning

CONNECT WITH
HAY HOUSE
ONLINE

🌐 hayhouse.co.uk   f @hayhouse

📷 @hayhouseuk   𝕏 @hayhouseuk

▶ @hayhouseuk   ♪ @hayhouseuk

Find out all about our latest books & card decks • Be the first to know about exclusive discounts • Interact with our authors in live broadcasts • Celebrate the cycle of the seasons with us • Watch free videos from your favourite authors • Connect with like-minded souls

'The gateways to wisdom and knowledge are always open.'

Louise Hay